THE DIGNITY OF
TRUST

NATHAN W. MCKIE, SR.

Copyright © 2024 by Nathan W. McKie

All rights reserved. No part of this publication may be reproduced, distributed, or transmitted in any form or by any means, including, photocopying,recording, or other electronic or mechanical methods, without the prior written permission of the copyright owner and the publisher, except in the case of brief quotations embodied in critical reviews and certain other noncommercial uses permitted by copyright law. For permission requests, write to the publisher, addressed "Attention: Permissions Coordinator," at the address below.

ARPress
45 Dan Road Suite 5
Canton MA 02021

Hotline:	1(888) 821-0229
Fax:	1(508) 545-7580

Ordering Information:
Quantity sales. Special discounts are available on quantity purchases by corporations, associations, and others. For details, contact the publisher at the address above.

Printed in the United States of America.

ISBN-13:	Softcover	979-8-89676-300-0
	eBook	979-8-89676-301-7
	Hardback	979-8-89676-302-4

Library of Congress Control Number: 2024922498

Table of Contents

PREFACE I

INTRODUCTION V
BACKGROUND VI
HIGH SCHOOL VI
COLLEGE DAYS VII
THWARTED PLANS VIII
FOUND: MY LIFE MATE IX
WHAT DOES DIGNITY HAVE TO DO WITH THIS? IX
WHAT'S THE PAYOFF FOR THIS BOOK? XI
THE CHALLENGE OF CONSIDERING TRUST XII
WHERE IS THIS HEADING? XIV

PART I THE IMPORTANCE OF TRUST 1
CHAPTER 1 How important Is Trust in Our Lives? 2
REAGAN'S CHARACTER 2
LEARNING FROM HISTORY 3
THE VINE AND THE HOLLY TREE 4
TRUST SPRINGS FROM TRUTH 5
THINGS REQUIRING OUR TRUST 7
CHAPTER 2 What Does It Mean to Trust Someone? 9
THE NECESSITY OF LEARNING TO TRUST 10
APATHY RULES 11
WORLDVIEW 12
OTHER COMPONENTS OF A TRUSTING RELATIONSHIP 13
TRUST AND OUR CULTURE 14

SOCIETAL ISSUES—LACK OF CONCERN 15
THE IMPORTANCE OF INTEGRITY WITH REGARD TO TRUST 16

PART II OBSTACLES TO TRUSTING OTHERS 18
CHAPTER 3 Poor Directions 20
CHAPTER 4 Detours 25
PRACTICAL EFFECT 25
GOOD OR BAD? 28
CHAPTER 5 Potholes 30
CHAPTER 6 Roadblocks 36
CHAPTER 7 Breakdowns 49

PART III WHAT TO DO WHEN TRUST IS LOST 57
CHAPTER 8 Overcoming Obstacles to Trusting 58
CONNECTING OBSTACLES TO MOTIVES 59
FLUSH OUT THE ROOT CAUSES OF THEIR MOTIVES 60
DEAL WITH ANGER ISSUES 62
SHOW CONCERN 63
LOOK FOR OPPORTUNITIES TO REBUILD TRUST IN SMALL WAYS 64
FOCUS ON POSSIBILITIES FOR SUCCESS 65
CHAPTER 9 Is It Really Possible to Restore Trust? 66
THE CHALLENGE OF RESTORING TRUST 66
SOMETHING NEEDS TO CHANGE 68
RELATIONSHIPS VS TRANSACTIONAL INVOLVEMENT 69
WHAT HAPPENS IF THIS DOESN'T WORK 70

PART IV CAN WE MAKE A DIFFERENCE? 72
CHAPTER 10 Is Our Trustworthiness Enough? 74
GOD AS THE SOURCE 75
BE A PERSON OF INTEGRITY 77
ADOPT A WORLDVIEW REFLECTING YOUR VALUES 79
HAVE THE COURAGE TO SPEAK THE TRUTH 80
HAVE COMPASSION ON THOSE WHO ARE IN NEED 83

MOST OF ALL, BE AN EFFECTIVE WITNESS TO YOUR FAITH 84
CHAPTER 11 Making the Connection to God 87
FROM TRUSTWORTHINESS TO DISCIPLESHIP 87
SEEKING COMMUNITY AS AN EFFECTIVE MEANS TO DRAW OTHERS CLOSER TO GOD 89
TRUSTING GOD TO HELP YOU LEAD OTHERS TO HIM 91
TRUSTING THE SPIRIT TO PRODUCE THE FRUIT 93
CHAPTER 12 Getting Beyond Self 95
WHERE IS COMMUNITY IN ALL THIS? 99
SO WHAT IS THE CHALLENGE? 100
APPENDIX A Jobs Where Trust Was Broken 105
APPENDIX B Two Real Stories about Trusting 109
REFERENCES 111

PREFACE

To the best of my memory, my first shot at writing a book began in the mid-1990s with an effort to provide wannabe entrepreneurs with some important information if they wanted to start their own business. I was in my early fifties and had been an entrepreneur several times over. The latest was essentially a spin-off from a manufacturer that I had been working for. I actually wanted to consult with the prospects after my first experience, but I realized that (1) most entrepreneurs feel like they have everything they need (except money) to make it on their own, and (2) they wouldn't have the money to pay me anyway. So, I put the idea on the back burner and went to work for someone else.

The more I started new businesses and kept getting slapped around, the more convinced I was that I had something to offer. The book that I wanted to write in the nineties was going to be about the pitfalls that await those brave souls who were determined to *do their own thing*. I actually drafted enough pages to fill a small book, but it was missing something. Most people don't want to read about a lot of problems that they might experience. They just want to jump in and start making money. Of course, it doesn't usually work that way. Success in small business is a very elusive commodity.

So, my next steps were in consulting. First, I was a business broker, which led to another business opportunity. The next was in retail, helping businesses raise money through promotions or to go out of business. In this book, you will find some of the issues that I had to deal with, which had nothing to do with whatever business I was in. Those experiences were why I ultimately decided to write this book.

Trust is extremely important to all of us. You can't get away from the need to be able to trust others. You can't even get in the bed and pull up the covers without having to be concerned with whether there is something that might go wrong. Wiring might short out and set your house on fire. Your dog might bite the mail carrier, and you could get fined or worse. You could get in your car to go somewhere, and it won't start. How do we navigate life's highways and byways without freaking out under the weight of all this pressure?

We are going to look at some ways to deal with this paranoia, but there aren't a lot of surefire solutions. I'm going to share my suggestions along with some other important points relating to trust issues. Many of us vacillate from not trusting enough to trusting too much. Finding that comfort zone in between is where we need to be.

There aren't a lot of people who I feel I can put my trust in. I've still ended up getting burned many times. P. T. Barnum, American showman and circus promoter, is credited with saying, "There's a sucker born every minute." He certainly should have known because he used many *hoaxes* in his performances. They weren't scams, though; he just wanted people to have fun. There have always been *hucksters*. *Merriam-Webster* says that these are people "who sell or advertise in an aggressive, dishonest, or annoying way." Now, that's someone I want to hang around with.

As I am writing this, there are some challenging things that I am going through. Being *betrayed* by people whom I thought I could trust is troubling me greatly. I make my feeble efforts at forgiving them, and then ask God to help me forgive. Some of the people who let me down were people who supposedly were all in on the proposed project. The first time I got a sense of where this was headed was when I put out a request for help demolishing part of the interior of the building we were taking over. No one showed up! It went downhill from there. When I was asked about what I needed from them, I told them that I needed volunteers and trainees to get prepared to be workers in paid positions. I got very few volunteers, even though the purpose of having them was to give them some exposure in the working world as Christians. The trainees came from various places, but only a couple came from the efforts of the church members. The whole purpose of this project was to help the local churches avoid drying up and blowing away. They just couldn't seem to get that *surviving* is not enough. It is hard to thrive when you are just trying to keep the lights on and keep the pastor paid (unless you have a volunteer).

So this *rant* is about trusting these churches to follow through on what they said they supported. I think this is indicative of what goes on in most churches today. My two previous books spoke of *call* and *service*. Most church members seem to forget (if they ever really knew) that "faith by itself, if it is not accompanied by action, is dead" (James 2:17, NIV). Instead, some Christians argue that this verse tells us to do something that is contrary to Ephesians 2:8–9 (NIV), which tells us, "For it is by grace you have been saved, through faith—and this is not from yourselves, it is the gift of God—not by works, so that no one can boast." Now, I'm not a bona fide theologian, but I have done enough study to know that these are not contradictory. Therefore, they are not a source of argument. Jesus even told his followers, as recorded in Matthew 7 (NIV): "Not everyone who says to me, 'Lord, Lord,' will enter the kingdom of heaven, but only the one who does the will of my Father who is in heaven" (v. 21). This is actually following a parable about false prophets where he was talking about the trees that bear good or bad fruit. He ends that section with this: "Thus, by their fruit, you will recognize them" (v. 19). Now, it does take some *connecting the dots*, but it is clear that the *will of His Father* is that we produce good fruit as evidence to our faith.

I will provide you with an understanding of how *trust* is important, what it means to trust someone, what some of the untrustworthy people are about, and how to be able to function in a world full of people who may not be that honest. On the other side of this, I hope to provide you with some ways to make it through life without losing faith in anyone or anything. That's not much of a life. Don't get too bogged down in this. You may even have some fun looking at the people who just can't stand to do things the right way. In any case, it is my desire that you become acquainted (if you haven't already) with the one true Source of trust.

INTRODUCTION

We all have probably had a *trust failure* at one time or another. It could have been by someone else, by us, or both. You may be thinking, "Not me!" In a narrow view of the term, perhaps we haven't. By that, I mean we really let someone down. We may have failed to pick up something at the store when we were asked to do so. It likely wouldn't rise to the level of *trust failure* unless it was medicine or something like that. For the most part, we would be forgiven for our memory not kicking in when it should have.

On the other hand, if we were supposed to pick up a child after school and didn't, there would be a mark on our record, so to speak. If we did that as a teenager, we might get grounded or lose driving privileges for a time. As adults, we might not get off so easily. In *Ragamuffin Gospel*, Brennan Manning writes about a man who was in an alcohol support group due mainly to the fact that he left his two-year-old daughter in the car in freezing temperatures while he was in a bar for several hours. The girl lost some of her toes due to frostbite. That was more than a trust failure—it was inhumane.

It wouldn't be true for me to say I have never been guilty of forgetting to do something that I was asked to do. My wife and I did leave our youngest son at the church once. It wasn't a major issue, though. We were going out of town and went by our house to pick up a few things. It was then that we remembered we had one less passenger than we were supposed to have. There were no tears or repercussions from it. Most of the incidents we were a part of wouldn't have involved trust.

My view of trust (or loss thereof) focused on someone intentionally violating their trust with another person or being involved in something that caused them to forget their responsibility. Perhaps I'm trying to excuse myself from criticism, and you can judge that for yourself. For my part, I have strong ethics when it comes to my family and those to whom

I have made a commitment. Further, I don't even care to capriciously do anything for which I could be judged to be untrustworthy.

Most of my life, I have been involved in some sort of sales position. There were a couple of jobs where I was responsible for performing some physical tasks on equipment that was part of my *tools*. It wouldn't have been acceptable for me to be lackadaisical about my responsibilities. I was out of town often, and I made sure that I checked on my family as I was traveling. I made sure that cars driven by my family were in good shape, especially when I was away. I could go on, but my point is that, I have done my best to be a reliable, responsible, trustworthy person for pretty much all my life. Being an only child probably contributed to that since there was no one else to blame for things that I did.

BACKGROUND

Now that I have tried to absolve myself of any accusations about my being a hypocrite, I want to lay the groundwork for the premise of this book. Maybe I will come up with some things that I did that rise to the level of untrustworthiness by the time I get to the end of this book. If that becomes the case, I will revise this session to reflect that revelation. Otherwise, it will still be here upon publishing.

There were some cases when I was growing up that I will skip because they didn't have a major effect on my outlook. What I want to focus on is a series of events that prompted me to address this topic as a part of a book. I will start with something that happened when I was in college and go from there.

HIGH SCHOOL

The schools I attended prior to college were small, and most people in the town where I was reared knew each other. That, of course, included knowing a lot about their business as well. I wasn't a particularly popular boy, but I was very loyal to those I felt connected to. Okay, I was probably a nerd. I made good grades and sought to excel in whatever I attempted. My parents were very interested in my learning how to be successful at tasks I undertook.

Boy Scouts was the first activity that I became involved in. Essentially, every boy in my small hometown was also involved. As I recollect, it was in that group that I was first disappointed by not being included in the advancement process. That made a big impression on me, and it has affected me for all my life.

It seems that I was almost more involved in relationships with adults and with teenagers in other towns when I went to high school. To some to others who aspired to achievement caused me to become more competitive. I think it was more a matter of seeking to better myself rather than to be *better* than others. Competition, if it is fair, can help to push us to greater heights. I believe we become our best when we are *committed* rather than just *involved*. In the case of 4-H Club activities, I won a district contest, three state demonstration contests, and a national demonstration contest. I was also a part of a state livestock judging team that competed in the national contest (it wasn't my finest hour, but a great honor nonetheless).

My mother pushed me to be involved in church youth fellowship activities and to become a counselor at a church camp. It was at that camp that I met the woman who later became my wife. I'm not one to be pushed into things, and my mother had ulterior motives for doing that to me. However degree, that was due to my involvement in many activities. In particular, the 4-H Club activities brought me into contact with people whom I wasn't involved with on a daily basis. I was asked by the county adult leader to be a part of demonstration events, and I jumped at the chance to broaden my horizons.

Being connected, I will always be grateful that she opened a door for me that made such a powerful impact on my life.

COLLEGE DAYS

While my academic achievements in college weren't stellar, the other activities made the experience a springboard to later life. My involvement in church youth activities led to my being chosen as the conference president of the youth fellowship. While in that position, I attended two national meetings. That helped to shape my spiritual life for years to come. It also made my choice of Carolyn Campbell to share over fifty years together the most important thing I ever did. Carolyn was the one whom I referred to in the previous section.

We were both counselors at the church camp and ended up working together with a group as co-counselors during the last week. One of the main things that stood out to me was that she was the only counselor asked to return from the previous summer. It was a testament to her character, and I was able to experience that during the summer we worked together.

At the time, both of us were *going steady* with other people. Everyone (including me) thought that I would be marrying the girl

I was dating upon graduation. We had been dating since high school, and there was an incident that strengthened our relationship. She had been involved in a car accident in a car her brother was driving, and I mistook my concern for her to be true love. I probably would have continued with that feeling had it not been for a series of events that made me lose my trust in her.

THWARTED PLANS

She began to take advantage of me, and I realized that I was basically her best alternative at that time. It was my choice to break up with her, and it was then that I learned the extent of her concern for me and my feelings. The realization that I wasn't going to have a future with her didn't come as the big shock that I thought it would. It seems to be human nature that we begin a backward look at our- selves when we hit a roadblock such as I had. The feeling I remember the most was that of being free of a burden. During the over fifty-plus years since then, my reflections on the event are still vivid in my memory. The betrayal that came after the better part of four years with her has colored my view of relationships in many ways.

It wasn't the first time that someone had *let me down*. It was, however, particularly painful since I had invested so much in the relationship. The notion of *discernment* wasn't in my lexicon until many years after that. The word has many synonyms, but judgment and perceptiveness stand out more to me than the others. *Intuition* is more about immediate reaction, and I certainly haven't been very good about that over the years. I learned a lot from my late wife about how to refine that skill, and I have shown some improvement.

The change of plans did affect my career path somewhat. With the previous relationship, lots of time had been spent making sure that my immediate plans after college were going to work. I was in the advanced Air Force Reserve Officers Training Corps, and this meant that I had a five-year commitment to the Air Force. Base housing, being around people whom we had never met before, and possible unaccompanied tours of duty didn't seem like the kind of life she wanted. She paid lip service to the notion, but it might have been our getting closer to the time for this to occur that made her interest wane.

FOUND: MY LIFE MATE

Carolyn and I were married and headed off to my pilot training experience in Lubbock, Texas. Neither of us ever regretted the decision to join our lives together. I don't think I could have been truly content with anyone else. I'm very glad I never had to find out. We produced three wonderful children and have nine grandchildren to add to that.

At this point, you may be wondering why I have put you through all the *soap opera-style* drama. Fair question. Well, it's not because I needed some catharsis. Learning to trust can be a drawn-out affair. British novelist Graham Greene once wrote, "It is impossible to go through life without trust: that is to be imprisoned in the worst cell of all, oneself."

Integrity has always been important to me, and trust is an extremely significant component of that. Together, we shared the pain of betrayed trust that others displayed, but she and I never wavered from the love and utter trust we had for each other. She suffered the same as I did, and I have sometimes thought that I was the real object of some things that she had to endure. I apologized to her for things that seemed that way, but she never backed off. I was at her side for support as she was for me. We were always in it together. Carolyn died on July 4, 2018, of a Parkinson's-type condition. It has been hard for me to handle many things without her, but I remember from where the strength we both had came: our Lord and Savior, Jesus Christ. I'm not sure how I could have functioned apart from that.

Dr. Charles Stanley, in a sermon about Noah entitled "Walking in the Favor of God," says that Noah provided the ABC formula for life: listen to God, trust Him, and obey Him. He went on to say, "To live a godly life, we must listen to God by reading His Word and trusting what He says. Then we step out in obedience, knowing that He has all knowledge and all power in every circumstance in life. Nothing is beyond Him. Furthermore, blessings follow obedience."

WHAT DOES DIGNITY HAVE TO DO WITH THIS?

This book is a departure, of sorts, from what I have previously written. While I always addressed the importance of *dignity*, I didn't really make it as personal as I am doing in this one. I like the definition that came up in Microsoft Word: "the state or quality of being worthy of honor or respect." The matter of being a *state* is something that is earned, and I think it is earned by having the *quality*. Being *dignified* is the act of behaving in a manner that makes us *worthy of honor and respect*. Sometimes, we don't act that way, and therefore, we are not worthy of it.

So, shouldn't *dignity* be something that comes and goes because of our worthiness at any given time? Bear with me on this: all three book titles begin with *The Dignity of*. So, in my view, when we create *profit* from a transaction or an event, or when we are in *service* to others, we have made ourselves *worthy*. Basically, what I am attempting to convey is that someone has chosen to consider being *dignified* as having achieved something.

If you have read anything I wrote or listened to me make a presentation, you understand the difficulty I have sometimes in writing/speaking in a clear and concise manner. I'd like to pass it off to age, but I remember, thirty-plus years ago, having a high school Sunday school class go, "What?" That would have been after a long, winding question that lost them somewhere along the way.

Can a person be considered *dignified* just because they act in a certain way? I don't think they can just because of the way they dress or behave according to social norms. My approach is one of helping others achieve honor and respect because they went beyond doing for themselves. Personally, I honor and respect people who help other people achieve *dignity*.

So, let's consider the premise in *Profit*. For years, I was involved in mission trips and food pantries, only to be frustrated and frankly annoyed. It was about the way we took away people's dignity by giving them things and doing things for them that they could and should do for themselves. In *Service*, Jeff Baker and I were looking to show others how *dignified* they become when they help people overcome the impediments to living a dignified life. The bottom line is this: serving people (at least the way it is commonly done) is not an effective way to move the poverty needle or to provide them with a sense of dignity. This would be the kind of honor and respect we all should get when we take charge of our lives and stop letting others give us stuff. Over however many years we have been building housing projects, we haven't seemed to get the point that people are not taking care of things that are given to them.

WHAT'S THE PAYOFF FOR THIS BOOK?

I hope you are not saying to yourself, "What?" You should rightly be asking what *trust* has to do with it. Here it is: when you betray a trust, you disrespect yourself and the person(s) you didn't show respect to. It means that you believe that you have the right to say/do whatever you want, and it doesn't matter how that affects others. Personally, it says to me that you have no respect for yourself or anyone else. Confucius once said, "Without feelings of respect, what is there to distinguish men from beasts?" It is difficult enough to get along in this world without there being respect for oneself and others. Yet we see rioting in many cities today and total disrespect for historical reminders with which we don't agree. We are seeing anarchy on a daily basis because people can't be trusted to make a decision. This seems to go from the lowest to the highest levels of our culture.

The late Christian apologist Ravi Zacharias commented on an article he had read in Canada regarding the thing that most teenagers wanted. The answer to the question was, "I just want someone to tell me the truth." How can we expect young people to be trustworthy if they have no trust in the adults that are supposedly leading the country? We have a large segment of the population who don't believe that there is objective truth. Frank Herbert, the science fiction writer, wrote, "Respect for the truth comes close to being the basis for all morality." Most of our laws are based on morality. Respect for others dictates that we create *rules* that enable us to get along with each other on the basis of fairness. In reality, we must also ensure that we provide the opportunity for all who are able to reach the highest level of achievement possible for themselves.

Jean Piaget, a Swiss psychologist best known for his work in child development, wrote of the need for rules in promoting child education. He said, "All morality consists in a system of rules, and the essence of all morality is to be sought for in the respect which the individual acquires for these rules." To take this further, *morality* embodies essentially all the elements we consider to be important in avoiding chaos.

For much of 2020, we saw chaos from groups that have nothing to do with COVID-19. While the origination was said to be of a racial nature, it is hard to see how that can be the driving force. Now, I'm not trying to say that there are no racial issues—far from it. However, for the most part, this is a problem that has been around for a long time.

The lack of trust is all around us in many disparate areas. There is essentially no trust with regard to how the virus got started or spread so fast. Since we don't trust corporate pharmaceutical companies, we don't trust much of what they say about vaccines and cures. Politicians have never been trustworthy in the eyes of most people, and it's on steroids at this point. In a study done in 2018 by Forbes, car salespeople and members of Congress were at the very bottom, and medical professionals were at the top. Since this was done in 2018, police were pretty high. The numbers that I saw showed high school teachers at 60% high/very high and clergy at 37%. Those are pretty astounding statistics! Given the way that the virus is causing many things to change dramatically, we may see some ratings shift around as well.

THE CHALLENGE OF CONSIDERING TRUST

The main reason I chose to focus on *trust* after two previous books is that trust is at the top of the list of most transactions. Any contract requires trust. Sure, the language of the contract provides the rules, but we all know that a lot of that is subject to interpretation. The heart of any contract is a *meeting of the minds*, and we try to achieve that. Later, I will share two instances in my current project that show the lack of enforcement ability that can send things sideways or worse.

Airing my *dirty laundry* is not what I am about, but I do have to bear some of the blame for a few of the things I have gotten into. Loyalty and a desire to believe the parties I am dealing with have gotten me in trouble more than a few times. Heck, I watch the true crime shows on TV and pull for people who I want to believe are innocent, even though I know they are guilty. I am an avid watcher of *Perry Mason* shows, and I try to get a sense of what people are up to. I have seen them so many times that I should have learned a few things. For instance, people who lie for no good reason are high on the suspect list. But then, there are people who lie to protect others or do so because they are afraid something else will be exposed about them.

My success rate is pretty good in matters where the facts are available. When I was a business broker, sellers of a business were worse than buyers when it came to getting a deal done. It was mainly how little they were going to get out of a transaction when the sale was consummated. Many of them wanted to smoke me with their version of the profitability and value of the company. I'll share some of those stories as well. There's always the matter of sellers feeling like the business was worth more than an objective assessment of it.

Speaking of facts, sometimes the truth may not square with the facts. "How can that be?" you ask. The reason is quite simple: the facts may not fit the situation. For instance, a person may be reporting income from the business that is reflected on an IRS filing, but there is other income that is being reported as something else. It may be legitimate, but it may also be taxable if it were reported as income. An example would be a company cell phone that is also used by the owner for personal calls. A broker would not normally make a big deal out of it, but large numbers of such transactions could raise a red flag. Also, the matter of trust may come into play if the potential buyer gets squeamish about transactions not being accurately reported.

It's pretty amazing what some business owners will do to take care of themselves and others who are close to them. Some of these can be very egregious, and they need to be acknowledged to avoid big problems later on. If they don't come up until the final negotiations are underway, the deal could crater right before your very eyes. I'm not trying to make a big case for how business transfers don't work out. However, there are many cases these days of mergers and acquisitions, and there are many other transactions that contain some of the same sinkholes as these.

I've been in court several times, but my only times as a defendant were when I was working for someone else. You can be sure that things can get out of hand very quickly in a courtroom. My biggest personal situation ended up with me losing, but then I got into it with my attorneys over unfulfilled promises. I managed to get out of it, but on balance, I would rather have avoided the whole matter altogether. The point is that you may get to where you don't know who to trust.

The worst ones that I have experienced were those that involved someone whom I felt I could trust completely. In the end, I pretty much lost out financially, but I also lost a relationship. The latest one ended up being tried in the court of public opinion. US Supreme Court Justice Clarence Thomas had to go through excruciating hearings when he was nominated. He said during the course of it that it was hard to prove a negative. I've thought about that many times. It's sort of like football players from opposing teams getting into a fight, and the one who took the first swing usually gets away with it.

WHERE IS THIS HEADING?

Again, I am not seeking pity or anything of the sort. I'm trying to do a couple of things:

1. Make readers aware of some of the traps that you can get into in any sort of situation.
2. Attempt to bring some semblance of sanity to the way we deal with others. The last thing I want to do is make things worse. If I can help people understand how much better life would be if we played straight with each other, then I will have become very successful at my goal.

I have sought input from many on this because I want this to be as comprehensive as possible. I think it is much more effective to learn from others, and that is my goal.

If we are prepared to trust relatively untrustworthy people at significant points in our lives—at the bank, on the bus, crossing a bridge, undergoing heart surgery—wouldn't we trust God?

—Alistair Begg, Christian pastor

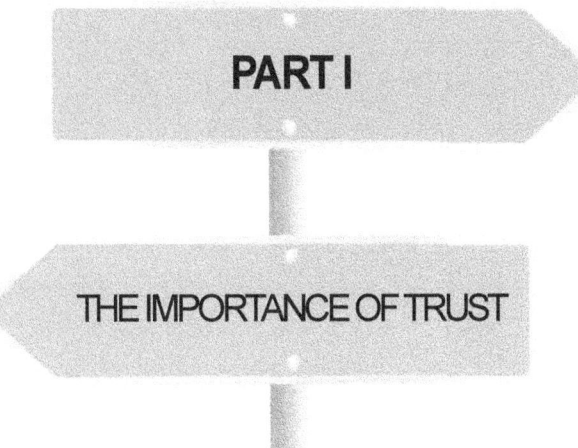

PART I
THE IMPORTANCE OF TRUST

When I decided to write this book, I was really trying to perhaps get something off my chest. You may have noticed that in the Introduction. As I considered the fact that this was the third book I have written, I looked to try to connect them. The *Dignity* factor was easy enough to connect with the first two, but I wasn't sure it was the case for *Trust*. However, as with the many messages I received, I came to realize that it made complete sense to include one of the most important aspects of developing meaningful relationships. The obvious extension then was *relationships are the basis for community building*.

From the very beginning, it was my plan to incorporate the three major areas of our lives: *creative, physical, and spiritual* (see www.luke16.org). Looking back (which is always a good idea if you want perspective), I came to realize that I had wandered into the almost-perfect connections to that with the three topics. All of them connect to the divine: creation to profit (producing fruit), physical to service (how we use our gifts to serve others), and spiritual to trust (how both of the other two help connect us to God).

As you consider *trust*, try to view it as the glue that holds all of it together as we live out our calling to spread the Kingdom of God. What more could be as *important* as having the Holy Spirit guide us as we do it?

CHAPTER 1
How important Is *Trust* in Our Lives?

Trust but verify.
—Ronald Reagan,
fortieth president of the United States

REAGAN'S CHARACTER

This quote from President Reagan came at a time when negotiations were underway between the Soviet Union and the US regarding the reduction and/or elimination of nuclear weapons. No one on the side of the US and its allies felt that the Soviets would ever hold up their end of the bargain. Reagan was able to make major strides with them, but his famous quote above shows how he felt that we should treat them.

Reagan's *Strategic Defense Initiative* (SDI) was a plan to create a shield of sorts around the US to be able to fend off a nuclear attack. It was very controversial and ultimately didn't reach fruition. It did, however, stir up concerns among the Soviets when they were considering the reduction of weapons. There are some statements to the effect that Reagan escalated the Cold War, and there were many actions taken in response to Soviet activity. The escalation began with the Soviet invasion of Afghanistan and President Jimmy Carter's decision to have the US Olympic team boycott the 1980 Olympics because of Soviet participation. It seems that Carter was too involved with the Iran hostage situation and also thought that his negotiations with the Soviets were going his way. At the end of Reagan's presidency, the Soviet Union had begun to crumble.

There were many other instances during that time when the Soviets were shown to be untrustworthy. Along with Margaret Thatcher, Prime

Minister of the United Kingdom, Reagan denounced the ideological motives of the Soviet Union. Keeping the Soviet's *feet to the fire* meant that Reagan was able to have a major role in the ultimate end of the Cold War, that also included several East European countries. Mikhail Gorbachev's election to the position of General Secretary of the Communist Party of the Soviet Union was certainly a catalyst for changes that enabled the end. The willingness of the Soviets to earn Reagan's trust truly proved to be the right position for him to have taken.

LEARNING FROM HISTORY

There is a saying: "What we learn from history is that we don't learn very much from history." This is very sad but also very true. In the world of politics, you can trust certain opposition forces to only want their supporters to hear the negative side of their opponent's actions. Earlier, I wrote about the matter of facts not fitting the situation. There are also times when headlines tend to rule the conversation. Just look at some of what is used to grab the audience, and you will likely find that there are many cases where the main body of information doesn't fit the headline.

When I used to sell instructional computer systems, I had to learn how the *courseware* (lessons provided in a software program) worked and could be used. Since it had been a few decades since I was in secondary school, and I was obliged to learn what some of the new things were all about. Specifically, there was one in the Language Arts curriculum that grabbed my attention. If you are as old as I am, you may not know what this area is. Well, it is the teaching of reading, writing, speaking, and listening. All these are important to being able to read, understand, and communicate the language.

One of the segments of this area was argumentation. This is not about people standing around shouting at each other in order to have their position heard. OK, it can be, but that is not what civilized people do in a classroom. Basically, it is about people speaking or writing something that puts forth the premise they want to be accepted by others. If you are able to discern whether the speaker/writer is putting forth an honest portrayal of the facts, you can then determine their sincerity. That, of course, doesn't necessarily mean that they are correct—that's up to the listener/reader to decide.

Let me put forth an example before you go "What?" and abandon this altogether. Once upon a time, reporters were cautioned to avoid putting their opinions into a news article that was supposed to be facts.

In those cases, *argumentation* doesn't play a part…or does it? *Bias,* the point-of-view side of argumentation, often becomes a *slanted* side of the discussion. Here's an example:

When Michael Brown was killed in Ferguson, Missouri, in 2014, the St. Louis County Prosecuting Attorney was Bob McCulloch. I personally witnessed McCulloch over the years I lived in St. Louis. Although his politics weren't much aligned with mine, I found him to be basically fair in his approach. However, when he took over the Michael Brown case, he was accused of being unfit to handle the case. McCulloch's father was a police officer who was killed while pursuing a kidnapper in a predominately black housing project.

It's not that this statement isn't true—it certainly is. However, the ones who wrote this into their reports were not in a position to judge whether McCulloch was unfit to be the prosecutor in this case or not. A prosecutor is supposed to be fair in their judgments, but we all have opinions, biases, etc. An idle statement, on its face, can change the conversation and sway opinions if they are inclined that way. If you want to believe that McCulloch was unfit, then a statement like this one would confirm your suspicions.

As this is being written, many protests have been carried out in major cities around the US. The vast majority of them have been in response to the death of a black man at the hands of the police. The subject is trust, right? So, seemingly, the point is that we don't trust police to engage a black man and not end up killing him. So, that is certainly not a fact, and therefore, the search goes on to find a reason for bias on the part of the officer who killed that man. The incident happened on May 25, 2020, and the call for defunding police and firing police chiefs goes on and on. Also, random shootings of police officers are taking center stage. So, what we have now is an abandonment of truth.

THE VINE AND THE HOLLY TREE

There was this well-developed holly tree at the corner of the front of our house in Des Peres, Missouri. It stood as a prominent figure in the landscape of our yard. Some friends of ours commented on the stateliness of the tree. Its evergreen nature withstands the elements to provide a colorful presentation all year long. Especially at Christmas, there is a reminder of how beautiful it is in spite of snow, frost, or ice.

I have fond memories of holly trees. When I was a child, I made a tree house in the holly tree in our front yard. My older brothers and others carved hearts in the bark. It was quite a history of former romances. It was also a testimony to the character of the holly tree. It seems that no matter how many names were carved in its bark or how many nails I drove in its limbs, it stood proud and tall in our yard. It was truly a monument to perseverance.

Holly trees are not uncommon. I remember many of them over the years. This particular one, however, had a special feature about it. The amazing thing about it is that no one seemed to notice. I certainly didn't until the second winter we lived in the house. I believe that this was the time that the feature manifested itself most fully. The "feature" I am referring to is a very large vine that was growing around the trunk of the tree. Now, it is not uncommon for vines to grow around trees or anything else they choose to. What was different about this one was its size and pervasiveness.

When I first noticed this vine, I was astonished at what I saw. I didn't realize it was a vine at first. The thing I noticed was that a section of the tree was dead in the winter. If the whole tree had been dead, or even the top portion, I would have suspected that the tree would eventually die completely. This section, however, was right in the middle. I found that to be very strange. As is the case with most of our lives, my busyness kept me from checking out the situation.

Finally, my curiosity got the best of me. I went out to give the matter a closer look. To my amazement, the vine was the same size as the trunk of the holly tree. It was wrapped around the trunk and went almost to the top. Its branches extended to the same length as the branches of the holly tree itself. Its leaves looked a lot like the holly's, and they had been about the same color when they were green. They even had berries like the holly had. The stark contrast at the time, though, was that it was not green. It was brown and ugly. It was not able to withstand the winter like the holly could.

TRUST SPRINGS FROM TRUTH

It's hard to say that just knowing what the truth is can be the basis for trust. In other words, if we get the truth, we can make an objective judgment as to whether you can trust the person about whom it is said. Another language arts component is *critical thinking*. With *argumentation*, we receive a series of statements providing a certain position on the subject. With critical thinking, we are asked to decide if the writer/speaker has made their case. So this means we have to make an objective decision about the subject as put forth by them. We can learn to trust the veracity of the position by verifying that their argument is correct. That may be difficult sometimes due to the lack of hard evidence. If you must make a determination of truth supporting the position, you just have to trust your experience, training, or your gut.

The point here is that truth is a wonderful thing to have. You are in a much better position to make a decision if you have the truth. So, how do we know what truth is? When Jesus came before Pontius Pilate when he was on trial for claiming to be a king, Jesus said He came "to bear witness to the truth" (John 18:37). Pilate's response was to say, "What is truth?" It wasn't really a question because he had his answer. In fact, he was illustrating a problem that remains to this day: whose truth are we talking about?

The dilemma for us is to determine whether we are talking about universal or relative truth. You may be thinking which I am talking out of both sides of my mouth. Actually, the point is universal truth is true for everyone, but relative truth may be different for different people. There are those who believe there is no absolute truth, and that would make all truth relative. The fact that the sun is hot is a universal truth. If there are people who hold the position that the sun is not hot, that doesn't make it true.

Relative truth, on the other hand, cannot claim universality. Where *relativism* fails is in thinking that their perspective, that is different from others, makes it true. The late Christian apologist Ravi Zacharias says, "Truth by definition is exclusive." In other words, if everything is true, then nothing is false. That simply is not true. There is no ground for *ethics* if truth is subjective. We can't, on our own, decide that our *truth* reigns supreme just because of our perspective. The lack of standards— those positions based on truth— causes us to live in a state of chaos. Standards cannot be subjective, and objective truths are true no matter what we believe about them. I recall that in past elections, the statement has been made that "you can have your own facts, but you can't have your own truth." This is a restatement of something I wrote earlier about facts not fitting the situation.

We will spend a good bit of time looking at *truth* because it is at the heart of *trust*. If people are not truthful, then it is difficult to have meaningful relationships. The lack of relationships means we can't have trust. There has to be a solid basis for people to be open and honest with each other. If you think in terms of how you relate to others, you can delve into how creating a bond can open things up to the point of vulnerability. Vulnerability requires trust since we can't use what we learn from others in a way that will damage how you relate. Not all your relationships will be as open as others, but you can be *real* to a great extent. This means avoiding phoniness that can derail your ability to relate effectively.

THINGS REQUIRING OUR TRUST

You probably don't get up in the morning and run through a list of things you need to trust during the course of your day. The list would be extremely long if you are like most of us. It would also drive you nuts just trying to determine how you can manage to get through a day without a million things going wrong. And yet, we must be able to be assured that much of what we rely on is going to work as it should. Let's look at a few of the things we need to trust.

Transportation. Whether we drive our own car, ride with someone else, or take some public transportation, we are going to face all sorts of potential perils on our way to work, or whatever it is we do with our time. Other people are hurrying to where they must go, just like you are. Drivers may not have gotten enough sleep or have something troubling them. Kids may be walking to school and not paying attention to what automobiles are doing. What about car trouble? Flat tires, stalled engines, faulty brakes—I could go on and on.

Family Matters. What if you and your spouse had an argument at breakfast? What's going on with your kids? Are they really going to school or skipping altogether? How are they going to function in the environment that exists in schools today? Is your mother-in-law coming for an extended visit or moving in permanently? Is your spouse having an affair?

Business Matters. Whether you are involved in a strictly business entity or just in an organization that has a public focus outside of business, you have responsibilities and pressures waiting for you when you arrive at the place where you work. Is the competition of working with others getting to you? Do you have a customer/client that is going to nail you for something you didn't do or did wrong? Is there going to be a layoff that puts you in a difficult situation?

Financial Matters. Unless you are one of the fortunate folks enjoying the luxury of plenty of money, you probably struggle with money matters one way or the other. Do you have "more month left at the end of your money?" Does the state of your finances weigh heavily on your mind? Are you getting collection calls from your creditors?

Health Issues. COVID-19 has made health a topic of great concern and discussion. At this writing, vaccines are being distributed, but many aren't interested in getting a shot. Have you had your vaccination? If not, do you plan to, or are you one of those who believes that it is not for you? We can't forget about cancer, leukemia, heart problems, etc.

Skilled Workers. Who do you trust to do work that you can't really see? There are a lot of occasions where work is not visible when it is complete: car engine repairs, construction (wiring, plumbing, concrete work)—virtually anyone who relies on the outcome to be satisfactory. I can tell you that there have been many instances of this work not being done well on something I owned.

This could go on almost forever. Beyond the areas addressed above, we have problems with personal business and relationships that cause us heartburn as well. For the most part, we have to *trust* that things will go as well as can be expected. Of course, they never do. The list above only barely scratches the surface.

How much better would life be if we didn't have so many things to worry about?

CHAPTER 2
What Does It Mean to Trust Someone?

Do not trust all men, but trust men of worth; the former course is silly, the latter a mark of prudence.

—Democritus

(ancient Greek philosopher best known for his formulation of atomic theory)

On November 14, 1978, US Representative Leo Ryan of California, a group of newspeople, and some relatives of cultists in a compound in Guyana landed near the compound. They were trying to find out just what was going on following allegations of mishandling funds. Close to a thousand members of the People's Temple had moved there from California. They were followers of Rev. Jim Jones, who had gotten these members to travel from the US to escape the scrutiny Jones and some of his leaders had come under. The next day, Ryan and fourteen defectors from the camp were assassinated while trying to board the plane. Jones ordered his followers to drink cyanide-adulterated punch, which most of them did. In all, 913 cultists (including 276 children) died, and Jones was found dead of a likely self-inflicted gunshot.

We all have some sort of gauge we use to make determinations about things. Some are more basic than others, but most of us feel this will get us by. As for me, I'm not always sure. Perhaps it comes from living in a lot of places and dealing with hundreds of people. In most situations, we can live with the outcome, but it's a lot more complicated than that.

It's been said we size up people we meet within a relatively few seconds. We look at others and compare them to ourselves or what we consider to be an ideal person for us to deal with. A bit scary, isn't it? I mean, what if we have to live with our decision? Surprise! We do. In many cases, our brain will do the work for us, and we don't have to obsess about the process. Lots of others feel that this is a pretty haphazard way of making such judgments. I've seen documentaries on the Guyana massacre, and I now know where the phrase "*drinking the Kool-Aid*" came from. It's really hard to understand why people would trust a person like Jones.

THE NECESSITY OF LEARNING TO TRUST

In Chapter 1, we looked at what it means to trust in today's world. There is a moral imperative for us to be able to trust one another at as high a level as possible. It could be as simple as the wrong soft drink coming out of the vending machine, or as significant as putting the wrong medicine in the bottle at the pharmacy. Sadly, if the person who puts the medicine in the bottle doesn't get supervised properly, the fault may lie with another person.

I often think of people who work for the government and make some monumental errors. If there is some payout settlement with the damaged parties, how many times does the person who made the error get held accountable? If the blame isn't properly placed, how does anyone ever learn how to perform better? Now, I'm not advocating for hiring more government workers, but there are some very important jobs that aren't being managed very well. Sometimes, I think we are just lucky most of the time.

TODAY'S LANDSCAPE

Somehow, we humans find ways to excuse our unwillingness to help others. The basic premise here is we let our mind guide us away from the real issue: compassion. We can conjure up all sorts of ways to avoid doing something for someone. It always infuriated me, when someone would start arguing with me when I suggested they do something outside of their comfort zone.

Many benevolent organizations struggle with this due to the lack of available funds. Robert Lupton, creator of FCS Ministries in Atlanta, has written two excellent books on how charity is best done. The premise is that we give people things when helping them do for themselves is a much better alternative. It's getting a bit personal to say that people who make decisions about helping the poor are not trustworthy. It's a fine line, to be sure, but Lupton has come up with a way to help people get out of poverty rather than perpetuate their dependency.

I have sat through many meetings about disaster recovery or attempting to help the poor that devolve into accusations that certain people aren't worthy of receiving aid. Where trust comes into play is twofold. We press every attempt to help by overdoing the response, or we begin to determine the level of worthiness in each situation. To some extent, *trust* is a factor, but mostly, we just evade the issue with a fell swoop. Just like the Black Lives Matter movement, we tend to avoid making meaningful progress toward a solution. If the *squeaky wheel* stops squeaking, we just kick the can down the road again.

There seems to be a whole host of organizations full of place-keepers. These would be people willing to show up at meetings for unknown reasons, but don't really have a clue as to how to work toward solutions. Most of them are not elected. Thankfully, at least, we aren't wasting money on people doing nothing. They are just not trustworthy enough for us to consider that they are accomplishing anything. It's not clear why such people agree to be on these boards. Someone they like and trusts their motives asks them, and they are now part of the wallpaper.

APATHY RULES

The sad reality today is that people really just don't care. We are so focused on ourselves that we miss the needs crying for attention. Everyone should be passionate about what they do. Otherwise, they will not have enough heart to be truly effective. I am certainly not naïve enough to think that every person with a responsibility can have the kind of passion needed to be trustworthy. Just a modicum of it would be amazing in most cases. It just seems to me that people with no drive or ambition can't really be trusted to carry out many tasks effectively.

To be fair, many people are victims of school systems and large organizations that just aren't wired up to help people make good decisions about hiring people. Some of it is due to the fact that many governments have made it too easy to get along without doing anything meaningful. People who are on some sort of disability in the US are not encouraged to do anything to benefit themselves or society. It's a thorny issue, for sure. On the other hand, efficiency and effectiveness in the workplace have been taking it on the chin for a few decades now. Those of us who are parents should probably know that children really want to make something of themselves. I remember feeling that I should find out what my life was supposed to be like when I was about twelve years old.

Today, there is a large segment of the population that just floats around from job to job or situation to situation without doing anything that would help them become truly productive in society. Drugs are a big factor, but all of it can't be blamed on that. How can we trust people to do the right thing when many don't even know what it means? We lack opportunities for socialization and involvement in community affairs. Sometimes, I get the feeling we are going backward in our efforts to become more than just a number.

WORLDVIEW

The best way I have found to make judgments about others is a single word: *worldview*. You may not be familiar with it, but *Merriam-Webster's* definition is "a comprehensive conception or apprehension of the world, especially from a specific standpoint." Basically, it is how we view the world. It's a bit like a *paradigm*. In other words, we are constantly making decisions about various aspects of living in our world. Once we come to a point of comfort with what is going on around us, we may decide to put a fence around our world. This, of course, means we exclude things that don't seem to apply to us. It may be OK for us to do this when our lives are simpler, a time when things seemed to make sense. As we grow, we need to take in more input to help us broaden our horizons or to revise our thinking regarding our existing positions.

This concept was introduced in *The Dignity of Profit*. The following is an overview of most of the points raised in that presentation:

1. Our positions are based on learning, experience, observation, and relationships.
2. *Paradigm shifts* occur when new information/knowledge is introduced into the existing paradigm, and we choose to change the way we feel about it.
3. Paradigms and worldviews aren't necessarily based on truth. G. K. Chesterton said that "truth is stranger than fiction because we made fiction to suit ourselves."
4. Having your facts right and fitting the situation (or result) is critical to being able to solve the problem you are dealing with.

5. Without a great deal of commonality in how the members of a group view the world around them, true community will be hard to achieve.
6. *Trust* may very well be the glue holding a group together. Without it, many things will be out of alignment, and forming meaningful relationships may be out of the question.

This is not to say that we cannot get along with each other if we don't have the same Worldview. That would make any kind of interaction between different groups very challenging. The important thing is to attempt to achieve that *meeting of the minds* I wrote about earlier. Failing in that, it might just be better to forego the matter altogether or go back and start over. Whatever is chosen is going to require a level of trust that both parties can live with.

OTHER COMPONENTS OF A TRUSTING RELATIONSHIP

Here is a listing of other important areas to include:

1. *Truth-telling*. Once again, being completely truthful with each other is critical.
2. *Follow-through*. Making sure that you provide the level of satisfaction that others deserve.
3. *Authenticity*. Being real is a must if others are to trust you.
4. *Loyalty*. While loyalty to one's supporters is the main issue, the agreement itself demands it as well.
5. *Realistic Expectations*. Staying within the boundaries of what the parties have agreed upon.
6. *An Absence of Malice*. Ensuring cordiality and respect will be a part of the outcome.
7. *Concern for the Rights of Others*. No healthy relationship can survive an unbalanced approach to making a deal work.
8. *True Friendships*. Characteristics: rewarding, accepted, loving, change (in good ways), intimacy at the deepest level, fruitfulness, security, spiritual growth (Dr. Charles Stanley).

Honor bespeaks worth. Confidence begets trust. Service brings satisfaction. Cooperation proves the quality of leadership.

—James Cash Penney, founder of the JCPenney retail chain

TRUST AND OUR CULTURE

Without a doubt, there are many issues that can create impediments to trusting relationships. Earlier, I mentioned the difficulty that exists in building trusting bonds. Without a chorus of supporters behind negotiations, being able to build trust requires time. Initially, we must learn to trust ourselves. Johann Wolfgang von Goethe said, "As soon as you trust yourself, you will know how to live." This trust is what makes us comfortable with who we are. If we don't believe we can be trusted, how can others trust us?

Walt Disney was once asked why he had villains in his cartoon shows. His answer was, "Without a villain, there is no hero." Today, it is hard to tell the villains from the heroes. One man's terrorist is another man's freedom fighter. Author Philip Zimbardo wrote a book entitled *Lucifer Effect: Understanding How Good People Turn Evil*. In it, he points out that we need to understand why people do such things, but we don't need to excuse it. The prophet Isaiah writes, "Woe to those who call evil good and good evil, who put darkness for light and light for darkness, who put bitter for sweet and sweet for bitter. Woe to those who are wise in their own eyes and clever in their own sight" (vv. 20–21, NIV). Many seek to overcome their aversion to sin by ignoring it. That only causes more problems. So, we have swerved into the matter of *sin*. Even church folk seem to have a problem with that one. It's been around since the beginning, but we try to avoid it because it bothers us so much. Zimbardo believes *power* is at the root of evil. Since sin is about disobedience, it's worth checking out the second part of the Isaiah scripture: "*Woe to those who are right in their own eyes.*" It took me a while to get the full thrust of this statement. It is so apparent today, that we miss the obvious. As I have worked to try to get people to work, many instances have arisen of people just not wanting to have anyone tell them what to do. If we go back to the notion of *worldview*, we can see how chaotic things would be if that were to become the norm.

Zimbardo also created a project known as the *Stanford Prison experiment*. You can check this out on Wikipedia if you want to know more about it. I happened on the video one day and was astonished. The object was to see how prisoners and prison guards behaved in a position of *perceived power*. I can't do this justice in a few sentences, but the outcome was not what anyone apparently expected. The power struggle got completely out of hand! He cites *seven social practices* that lead to becoming evil. These are not some crazy list of things most people wouldn't do. Taking the first step gets one involved.

SOCIETAL ISSUES—LACK OF CONCERN

From the story above, you can probably understand this is a very insidious process. There seems to be so much anger in our culture today; it's not hard to imagine people getting caught up in it. John Irving, an American novelist, said, "I think better of our behavior as individuals than I do when we see ourselves as members of a group. It's when people start forming groups that we have to watch our backs." This might not seem to square with the notion that people *do what is right in their own eyes*, but one of Zimbardo's social practices is blindly following others. However, people naturally tend to gravitate toward those who agree with them. It's just that madness seems to emanate from a mob mentality.

For the most part, we are talking about *tribalism*. Amy Chua and Jed Rubenfeld wrote in the October 2018 issue of *The Atlantic*, "When we think of tribalism, we tend to focus on the primal pull of race, religion, or ethnicity. But partisan political loyalties can become tribal, too. When they do, they can be as destructive as any other allegiance." To me, this is to be considered the normal course of things when we look at the nature of tribalism. It's been very interesting to me that people who might not really get along very well on a given day will readily rally around members of their group when outsiders try to make inroads into their *turf*. Although we don't hear as much about gangs these days, they still exist nonetheless. There are many groups, however, that exhibit tribalism in that they do things that can actually be harmful to the opposing groups.

Irving's comment about *watching your back* attests to the problem with forming a group or mob to try to get traction for your issues. In the late 1960s, there were protests over the US involvement in Vietnam. There were, of course, some substantive issues in it, but people were dropping out and forming communes for a variety of reasons. Of late, we have had the Wall Street sit-in and now protests over police brutality. Zimbardo would call these *crimes of opportunity*, which were essentially triggered by events that weren't particularly connected to each other.

I moved to a rural area in 2012 to try to get some economic life breathed into an area that had long since lost most of the businesses that once gave it some vitality. Factories and most of the natural resources were gone, but they weren't forgotten. Most of the residents felt they would be just fine if a factory would come in. Many attempts have been made to do it without success. There are a number of factors, but mostly, it is a sense of learned helplessness that I wrote about in *Profit*. It basically means that most people just don't care about what happens. The school district is the largest employer in the county, but without the childbearing families to repopulate them, this too will pass.

What is most amazing is that there is enormous tourist traffic, but there just isn't much interest by most locals in tapping into the revenue that could be realized from it. There have been some signs of life lately following the decision of a group to use some of the natural resources for events. Some of the businesses have responded to it, but the COVID-19 matter has kept it at a slower pace than would be the case otherwise. It's about the attitude of the cities (if you can call them that) that bothers folks like me. There just isn't much vision on the part of the general population.

Sadly, the majority of the local business activity comes from gasoline sales, auto repair, grocery stores, restaurants, and pharmacies. There are lots of churches, but their attendance isn't very good. This is the sad reality of most rural areas in the Ozarks and similar areas all over the country. My last real job was doing retail promotional sales for store owners who needed to raise cash or just go out of business. I have been involved with vocational rehabilitation groups, and they sing the same song—the '*we ain't got no jobs*' blues. Frankly, the jobs aren't there because people who live in these areas don't want them. People who do want jobs either commute to a nearby city or work outside of the area.

How can you develop a sense of trust in the place where you live if you are never there long enough to get to know the locals? With many schools closed or conducting classes remotely due to COVID-19, even sporting events that are usually connected to schools aren't happening. This phenomenon started in the 1950s; it's just getting worse due to population shifts and the pandemic.

THE IMPORTANCE OF INTEGRITY WITH REGARD TO TRUST

Integrity comes from the word *integer*, meaning "one way." The point is, we can't be duplicitous and be truthful at the same time. Being truthful is a foundational principle of a healthy society. It must be our duty to make every attempt to honor the truth and seek to ensure that people are truthful. Paul Meyer wrote, "By its very essence, integrity requires faithfulness, honesty, obedience, and more."

Taking this a bit further, people who travel the straight path of integrity are usually people who can be trusted. Later, we will look at how we can be prepared to deal with untrustworthy people. Being a person of integrity means we don't spend our time trying to work around some requirement we don't care for. Further, the rewards coming from being *one-way* are immense in comparison to whatever might be achieved by not being trustworthy.

We will address this later, but the traits of a person of integrity are all that is needed to find a person to be trustworthy. It is the kind of thing that needs to be a part of every organization and individual who wants to play in the *big times*. That is, the place where people only need the rules to back up what they would do naturally.

Up next: In Part II, we look at the obstacles we face while trying to determine how we can trust the people we deal with.

PART II

OBSTACLES TO TRUSTING OTHERS

For some time, I have felt there must be a lot of people who stay up nights trying to think of ways to trick other people out of their money. Maybe that is what these young people are doing rather than playing video games into the wee hours. Perhaps, but mainly they are playing games. It would almost be refreshing for them to be doing something more productive than living in a fantasy world.

The challenge in these chapters is to keep from going on and on about all the things fraudulent people are coming up with these days. A lot of this is not new; even in the book of Genesis, tricksters were working to put something over on someone.

As the front cover suggests, we are looking at this as if we were trying to steer ourselves through all the *obstacles* we may face as we live our lives. In *The Dignity of Profit*, we offered an acrostic we ultimately used in our project described in the book. This was REACT: recruiting entrepreneurs to assist communities to thrive. Our objective was to create an organization that helps train and support budding entrepreneurs so that they could be successful. We readily recognized business as just one of the components of a balanced lifestyle. The parent organization of REACT is Luke 16 Corp. It is a 501(c)3 nonprofit enterprise, and this concept is described on our website, www.luke16.org. If you will take a look at this site, you will learn how we convey our understanding of making sure all facets of our existence run at a highly efficient pace. This means avoiding the obstacles that sidetrack us.

Most of what will be presented here is either from personal experience or from stories that have been shown to illustrate just how we must prepare ourselves for this journey we must take. This is not unlike our approach in *Profit*, but it delves deeply into the matter of trust.

The assumption being made is this: we are familiar with the challenges of venturing off into the uncertainty of a new venture or course of action. I use common terms to describe the categories that face us—with increasing complexity.

CHAPTER 3
Poor Directions

I believe it is a Chinese proverb that says, "The journey of a thousand miles begins with one step." That first step can be critical in order for us to be headed in the right direction. Some people—not you, of course—just take a shot at determining what route to take to get to their destination. I'm not talking about relying on a GPS, although it's not a bad idea to get a general sense of landmarks that you can look out for along the way. I have had more than one experience where my GPS led me astray.

So, stretching our metaphor a bit, let's consider how we can get headed in the wrong direction by getting *poor directions*. Men are particularly known for not wanting to ask directions from others. I know, it's that *control* thing. Well, that's not always true. Since I am one of those folks who doesn't like to waste anything (OK, I'm cheap), I hate to waste my time and gas chasing rabbits—or wild geese. Therefore, I will stop and ask locals for directions. The problem I have is that some places have names for highways, etc., not shown on a map that way. Also, some people will give you landmarks like *farmer Brown's cow in a certain field*. I'll let you figure that one out.

When I first was making sales calls in New York City, I had a terrible time making sense of the directions I got from internet websites. On my first foray into the city, I mistook one exit for the one I was supposed to take. If you know anything about the city, you know there aren't a lot of ways of getting across the Hudson River from New Jersey (west side). After taking the exit I thought I was to use off the George Washington Bridge, I found myself on the west side of the Hudson. I couldn't figure out how to get across to the east side from there. I knew I was going to be late for my appointment, so I called my prospect to see if he could give me any guidance. He quickly told me he used a GPS and didn't have any idea how to help me. When he told me I should stop and ask someone in the area, I knew I was in trouble. You see, I had ended up in Spanish Harlem, and I didn't see any signs in English. I won't bore you with the details, but I did get out of there by going much farther north. I got a GPS before I went into the city again.

While poor directions can sometimes be disastrous, my purpose here is to use them as the lowest level of *mistrust*. In these cases, I make the assumption that it is a lack of competence or concern that makes the information from your source unreliable.

False Promises. Again, I'm assuming that having this as a response from someone is they mean no harm. Suppose you ask someone to go by your house and see if anything looks out of order while you are out of town. The person may agree to do it, but it is just not on their list of important things for them to take care of. This could be a minor issue, but it might be the beginning of your not wanting to trust the person the next time you need something done.

Unrealistic Expectations. This might be something a person really thinks they will do, but they probably won't because of certain factors. Let's say a person asks you to buy a lottery ticket for them and says they will give you some percentage of the winnings if it is a winner. Depending on the veracity of the ticket holder, this may or may not be a *realistic* promise. After all, the chances of winning are quite small. What happens if they win and refuse to live up to their pledge?

Ego Defense Mechanisms. This analysis of what makes people bogus is not intended to dig very deeply into psychological matters, but clearly, most of what triggers our reactions to an external stimulus evokes a psychological response. Sigmund Freud is very well known for his study of the ego, so it makes sense to consider the defense mechanisms he describes. These are the ways we deal with difficult matters that cause us to struggle over how we are going to behave. To avoid getting too technical, let me give a basic statement of what happens to cause this struggle.

Freud has used terms to describe the two opposing poles of our ego. The *id* is the pole that could be considered to be the "devil on our shoulder." The *superego* is the term he uses to describe the "angel on our shoulder." When a situation arises that doesn't clearly fit one or the other of the poles, we unconsciously use one of the defense mechanisms to move the situation to another place, so to speak. These act like *mediators* to keep the peace. This the role of the ego.

There was a time in college when I thought I wanted to make psychology my major. I have always been fascinated by the actions people take and why they do what they do. My wife helped me to come to my senses by making the point that many people get into psychology because they have problems themselves. I don't mean to suggest that all psychologists are people with problems; I just mean I don't have much patience with people who don't seem to get it. However, one of the reasons I have been fascinated by all this is I spend a lot of my time trying to analyze my motives and those of others.

- *Denial.* *Denial* is a word that can be interpreted in a couple of different ways. If you are in denial, you are causing your own problem. This would be like refusing to accept some fact that is actually true. Perhaps you don't believe a tornado is moving across the path you are planning to take. Another case would be when someone denies doing or not doing something that is going to cause you some heartburn if you accept their denial as truth. A blot on their character, for sure.
- *Displacement.* You direct strong emotions and frustrations toward a person or object that doesn't feel threatening to you. This allows you to satisfy an impulse to react, but you don't risk significant consequences.
- *Intellectualization.* When you're hit with a trying situation, you may choose to remove all emotion from your responses and instead focus on quantitative facts.
- *Projection.* This is another way we try to redirect our attitudes about the truth; we *project* it on someone else.
- *Rationalization.* Some people may attempt to explain undesirable behaviors with their own set of *facts*. This allows you to feel comfortable with the choice you made, even if you know on another level it's not right. In *Service*, I called this *rational lies*. To me, we are masters at talking ourselves into or out of a certain position to one we can live with. It doesn't take us too many steps down that path before we can justify to ourselves (and maybe others) that we are correct in believing what we want to believe. Most of the time, it doesn't make sense to others, but we can buy into it at some level. It may be buying something you can't afford or skipping an event you really don't want to go to. Neither of those is a big deal in most instances. However, matters like this can be the beginning of a ride down a slippery slope.

- *Reaction Formation.* People who use this defense mechanism recognize how they feel, but they choose to behave in the opposite manner of their instincts.
- *Regression.* Some people who feel threatened or anxious may unconsciously "escape" to an earlier stage of development.
- *Repression.* Unsavory thoughts, painful memories, or irrational beliefs can upset you. Instead of facing them, you may unconsciously choose to hide them in hopes of forgetting about them entirely.
- *Sublimation.* This type of defense mechanism is considered a positive strategy. That's because people who rely on it choose to redirect strong emotions or feelings into an object or activity that is appropriate and safe.
- *Compartmentalization.* Separating your life into independent sectors may feel like a way to protect many elements of it.

So, at this point, I would ask you to join me in considering what these *mechanisms* have to do with trust. Frankly, the more I have thought about this, the more I find it is very much about trust. Let's take *denial,* for example. One definition is *"refusal to admit the truth or reality of something (such as a statement or charge)."* This has a number of different connotations, but *refusal to admit the truth* can put a serious roadblock in the way of trusting someone. If you have a five-year-old child who denies having eaten a cookie that is missing from the lot, you have the opportunity to take advantage of a *teachable moment.* I'm not naïve enough to think this is a *one-and-done* situation, but you can deal with it when it comes up again. At that point, you can decide if punishment is appropriate. Heck, there are adults who deny such actions, and you can determine if this is a hill to die on.

When I was just learning to drive and didn't yet have my driver's license, some friends and I decided to go for a *joy ride* one night when my parents were out of town. I *rationalized* that I could drive safely, and there would be no harm to come from my actions. My friends and I rode for a few miles and decided we should turn around. It was a rainy night, and the right front wheel slipped off into a muddy ditch. There was no way we were going to be able to get it out on our own. Fortunately, we weren't far from the house where my dad's farm manager lived. I slopped down the mile or so to his house in the rain. He was a wonderful man, and he would have done anything I asked—within reason. He pulled us out with his tractor, and we went on our way home.

Since I didn't have my license, my parents were not expecting me to take that drive. My secret is secure to this day, except that perhaps my parents in heaven may have had the benefit of some *old home movies* that God keeps. While they were alive, however, none of us spilled the beans. By the way, when I arose the morning after the *incident*, I found the manager washing off the mud from the wheel that went into the ditch.

While my parents never seemed to know about my misdeeds, there were times when I wasn't too sure. Conscience is a powerful part of our psyche. Every time I did something I knew I shouldn't have, I would get the feeling I really wish I hadn't down in my gut. See, the other part is having children causes you to see that movie run over again. I always wondered whether my parents just let it go to torment me, or they really didn't have a clue. One thing I was pretty adamant about was not doing something that would reflect negatively on my parents. I had great respect for them, although it didn't always seem that way. I knew I could trust them to always do the right thing for me, and that is why I didn't want to disappoint them. I do believe my conscience helped keep me from getting off on the wrong track.

It's pretty interesting that, unlike parents, God knows everything we do. If we do things with full knowledge that God is aware of them, what does that say about our trust in God? Well, first of all, it shows a definite lack of respect—we just don't care. So, how do we feel about the possibility of consequences? What if there don't seem to be any? Wow! Could it mean that God doesn't care? This is getting a bit deep theologically. My understanding is that God does care, but if we don't, maybe we are left to our own devices. Now, that is a scary thought!

All this has to do with whether we can become trustworthy or not. These *ego mechanisms* can definitely throw a curve in our ability to become a trustworthy person. General Robert E. Lee once said, "I cannot trust a man to control others who cannot control himself." Self-control is vitally important, but it is ominous to consider how that works. Perhaps you have experienced this one way or another. Weaknesses can control us. When we use those *mechanisms* to deflect from the truth, we don't really have much control, do we?

CHAPTER 4
Detours

On the road of life, we all have detours. These are things that come up when we are on the way to doing something that seems to be very important. In the bigger scheme of things, most of them are actually not important. In many of those cases, we get all worked up over something that gets under our skin. Sometimes, we let these distract us from our true purposes, and we pay some sort of price for it. I firmly believe that God puts detours in our lives so we will be prepared for what He has in store for us. Dr. Tony Evans did a series of sermons on this topic, and the central character was Joseph. You remember Joseph; he was a member of Jacob's tribe who got sold into slavery in Egypt. In the end, Joseph ended up saving his family, even after they had wronged him so badly. That's not what I am referring to. The detours that cause us to be untrustworthy are quite different from that story.

PRACTICAL EFFECT

Delays. This could be just a matter of procrastination. On the other hand, it could be that we have no intention of doing what we have said we would do in the first place. So what we really do is keep dragging our feet until the feeling goes away, or the person we made a promise to hopefully forgets about it. As a salesperson, I have had many people drag me along when I expected them to follow through on what they said. For a long time, it has been my practice to be upfront with people or to at least avoid making a commitment I can't follow through on. I'm always shocked when someone praises me for doing something they surely were expecting me to do. To me, it's just good business, and it is especially important in gaining and/or keeping people's trust.

Changes in Plans. This, of course, could also be something that is unavoidable. In such cases, we should be sure to be truthful about why we are making changes that affect others' plans. It is another matter if we just didn't want to say no in the first place. The reason this is in the category of a *detour* is it may just be an inconvenience, and most people will likely let it go. However, if it is a malicious lack of consideration, it might very well rise to the level of causing a rift between you and the person(s) you have offended. My feeling has been that such insensitivity is a pretty big sum to pay for the loss of a friend or even their trust.

A Sense of Urgency. People may impose a sense of urgency on you, or you may suddenly realize that you need to get something done right away. Let's say you are getting ready to go somewhere when you are reminded that you need to take your dog outside to do his/her business. In most cases, I have found, your dog doesn't have the pressure of time you do. Additionally, you might have a mishap (like stepping on something) or discover something else that you need to do before leaving. My guess is you have had this happen—maybe on multiple occasions. When I work out of my home, I find this to be all too often. You would think that I would learn. However, the many things on my mind become disturbed by this activity.

So now what? Your detour increases the sense of urgency you had before. When that happens, you tend to make mistakes, or you have to try to explain away the reason for your lateness to someone. If you are late to a doctor's appointment or to a meeting with a client, there are ways to learn to avoid it if at all possible. Friends may forgive you, but my late wife was perpetually late in picking me up at the car repair shop or whatever. I learned early on that I had no recourse in this, and I just decided to put something between my teeth to keep from grinding them to a nub. She was a very lovable woman, and I think most people forgave her for her tardiness. On the other hand, getting distracted and not getting a task done that someone was expecting quite often caused her some problems.

Insincere Motives. There are some people who just do things to other people out of meanness. I don't know why they do it; they just can't help themselves, I suppose. Whatever the reason, most people are pretty annoyed when they get treated that way. They may try to retaliate, or they may decide that life is too short to get worked up over such pettiness. There are some people who are practical jokers and feel that other people find such antics as funny as they do. Perhaps this is not so much a matter of trust as it is an alienation that is probably justified. Putting up with such behavior is a detour that can be easily avoided. Just don't associate with these people. Let others deal with them, or just ignore them and forget it.

Nominal Adherents. The word *nominal* basically means "*in name only.*" Many people show up in church and profess to be Christians, but their life doesn't show it at all. You may have heard that "sitting in a church expecting to become a Christian by that alone, is like sitting in a hen house and expecting to become a chicken."

Such behavior has also been called *practical atheism*. It's a toss-up as to whether this belongs in the *potholes* section or here. It all depends on the nature and extent to which a person might go. In other words, being something other than what you purport to be means you are not true to one or the other. If you are essentially *nominal*, you are probably not in a position to be a source of good information about what you profess to believe. People join groups for a variety of reasons, and some of them are not good. Anything worth being a part of is something you need to believe in and seek to make it all it can be.

There are several different designations for those who aren't *all in*. There are some who are simply *intellectually* assenting to be a member, and they may even regularly attend a service, meeting, or whatever goes on in the basic activities. As far as most Christians go, 98 percent of their time is involved with things that have nothing to do with their church life. You can do the math if you like, but it is not hard to reach that number. It's not possible to know what is going on in people's brains, but people who are honest about it will agree that their lives fit more into the nominal category than *devoted*.

As a resident of a certain area and a consultant who spent extended periods of time in different places, I was either a member or regular attendee of at least twenty-four churches. During those times, I found very few of them who even gave the impression of being engaged in their community. Even the current bishop of the United Methodist Church in Missouri once wrote about the fact that most churches were just "playing" at it. There are no statistics I know of to categorize the level of devotion a person has to their church or organization. However, in a great book entitled *Church on Sunday, Work on Monday: The Challenge of Fusing Christian Values with Business Life* by Scotty McLennan and Laura Nash, it describes the gap between how people can compartmentalize their faith and their work. This study included many clergy and laity and addressed both sides of virtually every aspect of church life. In the end, there wasn't much accomplished in the way of progress. Neither side seemed willing to budge.

Jealousy. Proverbs 27:4 (NIV) says, "Anger is cruel and fury overwhelming, but who can stand before jealousy?" When I wrote *The Dignity of Profit*, I pointed out how lethargy, apathy, lackadaisicalness, and anti-capitalism (L.A.L.A. land) can help kill efforts to make meaningful progress toward success in a venture. Once I got into a project where we were trying to improve the economic climate of an area, I realized that *jealousy* and *complacency* were just as prevalent as the others. Complacency might be included as part of the original ones, but jealousy is another matter. The problem with it has to do with the insidiousness that can be a part of it.

Let's say that a person gets to do something that you wanted to do. You may be disappointed, but you weren't really obsessing about it. What if, though, in your inner being, you couldn't let it go? You may not even be aware of how badly you were feeling about it. However, given the chance, you might subconsciously look for ways to thwart the plans the person had to do. There are cases where people go to extreme measures to hurt the other person.

The practical effects of jealousy might be that it goes beyond the *detour* stage and could even bring the person to ruin. In my last project, there was a person who tried to get the media involved to undercut our efforts and threatened to complain to the IRS. We were able to get through the requirements of the grant we received, but we had to walk away at the end of the initial project due to his poisoning the marketplace environment. He essentially derailed the efforts to improve the community. More on this in chapter 6.

GOOD OR BAD?

There have been many *detours* in my life. The first one I remember was the one I told in the Introduction—the girl I thought I would be marrying. My mother claims credit for that one turning out so well. She claimed that she prayed every day that I wouldn't marry the girl. Maybe that's true, but in any case, I do believe I needed some time to learn about life before I met my *real*-life mate. I've had a lot of detours in my working life as well. There is a good bit of detail in Appendix A if you care to check it out. You can decide if those were detours or just bad judgment.

You may be familiar with the series of questions that starts with "How do you get *wisdom*?" The answer is "From good judgment." The next question is, "How do you get good judgment?" The answer to that one is "From bad judgment." That seems to describe what detours are meant for if they are for the right reasons. It used to frustrate me when God seemed to be behind this scenario. Now I have learned that, if I will trust Him, He will orchestrate these matters (see Proverbs 3:5–6). More on this later.

CHAPTER 5
Potholes

To keep this metaphor of being on a journey, our next step down the list of obstacles is *potholes*. In the real sense of driving, potholes can be very damaging to a car, and they can be a real bother to drivers. If you blow a tire, you can be stopped in your tracks—at least temporarily. On the other hand, if you knock your steering out of alignment or bend a wheel rim, you can potentially keep driving for a while. It's not a good idea to drive very long because the damage to your tires will only get worse.

Well, you might be thinking this is good information, but what does it really have to do with trustworthiness? In the beginning, we talked about things we trust. If there is a problem with your steering or with your life/business, the effect can be the same. Inattention to the problem will quite possibly lead to bigger problems. So, let's look at some of life's potholes and their effects.

Scams. First, we will look at the most common categories:

- *Advance Fees*. Paying a deposit or fee to secure some arrangement that you are seeking to have with the person. Much of the time, this is either a way to extort money or start a job and not do nearly as much work as has been paid for.
- *Computer Hacking*. Giving access to your computer to someone who has promised something in return. Much of this is simply to get your information for purposes of financial gain.
- *Charity Solicitations*. This can range from outright donation requests to the sale of items or tickets that are allegedly for some needy group.

- *Credit Card and Banking Scams.* These are usually designed to get your account information and, hopefully, your social security number. No reputable organization would ask for this without providing you with the kind of protection you need.
- *Small Business Scams.* Owning a small business makes you particularly vulnerable since funds are usually tight. Special deals on anything from light bulbs to credit card processing fees to advertising opportunities are ones that should be suspect.
- There are far too many different versions to try to list, but here's one that I was personally aware of. When I was in the Air Force, I was stationed in a small city where there was a highway running by on the edge of town. There were three *service stations* (I use that term because they did repairs and maintenance as well as pumping gas). These stations got together and created a scam that each was a part of. Two stations were located on either end of the highway coming into the city. When they checked under the hood of a car getting gassed, they would spray silicone on the alternator. After they left the respective station, the alternator would fail—just about the time it reached the station in the middle. A bit of collusion can mean big problems for the unwitting victim.

With the internet being as pervasive as it is today, it is a small wonder there are so many scams. Most of what is listed above has to do with money. There are many others involving people's lives, even though they also involve money. Human trafficking is rampant in our world today. This is especially true of girls in their teens as well as young adults. Many of them are lonely or wanting to get away from a home life that is not safe. There were three hundred of them kidnapped at one time by a terrorist group in Africa a few years ago.

There was a movie about what happened to girls in Bosnia after the Balkan War. This was involving US military members. Even if they are not kidnapped, they may be enticed into a situation where they don't feel that they can escape.

I've always found it difficult to understand how people can be so gullible on one hand while being so careful about other things. The few people I have engaged in conversation say the perpetrators have a way of being convincing while being manipulating. After they find themselves in a difficult situation, they wish they had been more discerning. Unfortunately, by that time, it is too late for many of them.

Outright Lies. John Wesley once wrote that there is no such thing as a *little white lie.* He felt a lie is still a lie, although it might not be as egregious as some others. The main criterion to many is that something we tell that is not exactly true but harms no one else is really okay. There is no such thing as a victimless crime, and there is no false statement that only hurts the one issuing it. In any case, it is a black mark on our conscience that can affect future events as well. In one sense, there are lies quite damaging to others, and some might just be an indicator of what a person's character is really like. I have been the managing consultant for the nonprofit mentioned earlier in this chapter. While the objective of this organization was to help people who had gotten to the point where they were probably beyond help, I wanted to try to give them a helping hand. Many people told me not to do it, but telling me no just makes me want to do something all the more. At least four of the residential tenants just couldn't tell the truth to save their own souls. One of them never followed through on anything he promised to do. I still have the stream of text messages revealing just how far he went.

The man in the story I just related has left a string of lies and destruction in his wake. As bad as that and other instances were, these do fit into the *pothole* category to the extent that they are, at least, a jolt to your willingness to trust people. We will see later how *lies* fit quite well in some categories that do have a very significant effect on others.

Shams. These are basically fake events or falsely presenting something as the truth. Something that is well-known as a *sham* is a pillow cover by that name. You probably know what that is; you can buy a set of bed covers that includes it. You can take a pillow that has SpongeBob on it and stick it inside the cover, that makes it look great—matching all the rest of the covers. Other words that describe this are *bogus, fraud, hoax, and counterfeit.* Sometime back, I was thinking of writing a book that I was going to call *Somewhat Bogus.* Of course, there is nothing that can be somewhat bogus because you either are or you are not. It's sort of like being somewhat pregnant—it's not possible!

The Bible has quite a few of these. None of them were acceptable to God, but there were consequences to all of them. Abraham tried to pass his wife as his sister to avoid having problems with Abimelech. Jacob and his mother tricked his father, Isaac, into giving Jacob the birthright that was customarily due to Esau. Joseph tricked his brothers in Egypt into bringing the family, thereby not revealing who he really was. These are all recorded in Genesis, but there are several that didn't turn out so well. The point is that God worked these out to serve His purposes.

I suppose this could be akin to the *wolf in sheep's clothing* category. These folks are just simply hiding who they really are. There are other terms for this, but the idea of being *undercover* seems to apply here. It's not clear whether people are really just hiding or if they are putting on a front in order to avoid being found out.

There are many ways this can play out. There was a man in St. Louis who suddenly disappeared. He had started a company and went to New York to see about getting some funding for his company. When he disappeared, his clothing and virtually everything else he had with him on the trip were in the hotel. His wife was left in St. Louis to deal with the fallout of not being able to pay bills and to face the uncertainty of what had really happened. As it later turned out, he and his wife were found living in east Tennessee, pretending to be father and daughter. He was selling tourist rentals or something like that.

Sophistry. This is tricking someone by making a seemingly clever argument in order to convince you that it is correct. It is basically twisting the truth to make it fit one's needs. My belief has been if the truth is not compelling enough to convince others, it is better to go for being truthful. In the end, it will mean people trust you more.

In this case and in the next one, *argumentation* is used to make the case as opposed to the truth. Mortimer J. Adler said, "Too many facts are often as much of an obstacle to understanding as too few. There is a sense in which we moderns are inundated with facts to the detriment of understanding." In the case of *sophistry*, we have people using false arguments by adding facts that don't fit the situation itself. The next case is one in which the argument just *sounds good.*

Here is an interesting quote used extensively to support the notion of *sophistry:* "But Keynes smoothed over the harsh Marxist anti-individualism with artful sophistry and clever rhetoric into something salable to Americans." In *Profit*, I wrote about John Maynard Keynes and his belief that government should be in control of the economy (OK, that may be reaching). My point is not to debate that at this point, but I simply want to show that it illustrates how argumentation works. I believe the quote is accurate, but I can't prove it. In fact, both sides of the argument have valid points. I don't want to be accused of sophistry when I can't be absolutely sure of the veracity of my own argument. In case you are wondering what this has to do with anything, I just want to show that our point of view may be overshadowing the possible correctness of the other one.

Specious Arguments. Perhaps it would be good to define the word *specious* before we seek to understand its use. Basically, it means "superficially plausible, but actually wrong or misleading in appearance, especially misleadingly attractive." Just think about it: don't you know of occasions when you or other people have done just that? If we don't invest the time in learning about the thing that we have an opinion on, aren't we really doing more to damage ourselves than anyone else? It's too bad we have to be so suspicious about what people tell us, but it goes beyond whether a person is trying to be untruthful or not. After all, people don't particularly like to be on the weak end of a discussion or a negotiation. Therefore, they tend to embellish their position in order to appear stronger.

Hypocrisy. This is a term batted around in many different arenas. The definition in Dictionary.com is "a pretense of having a virtuous character, moral or religious beliefs or principles, etc., that one does not really possess. a pretense of having some desirable or publicly approved attitude." My personal opinion on this is that hypocrisy is one of the most disgusting things we find in our culture today. The New Testament is full of criticisms of hypocrites, as are many other writings.

Most people seem to understand the nature and practical effects of hypocrisy. It is probably one of the best-known causes of distrust to many. When you think about it, how in the world do you trust someone who is basically a phony? Even if they sometimes act in a manner consistent with their words, it is hard to know when they are genuine. This is quite different from the other ways we might find misleading or outright lying. All of us are probably guilty at one time or another of one the others. However, when we act hypocritically, we are, in effect, causing others to label us in ways that make our opinions and attitudes suspect.

After I closed my manufacturing business, the inventory was sold to a supplier who contracted with me to be the marketer for the materials to my former customer base. Many businesses find this to be an easy and profitable way to make a business transfer. For me, it was a way to get into a more profitable line of work while still benefiting from the new relationship that had been formed. The arrangement worked pretty well, except some of my customers weren't comfortable with the change. Things went along rather smoothly anyway until the owner of that business died. While the contract lived on with the new owner, the relationship we had was not the same.

One day, I got a call from the new owner, who wanted to understand the nature of the contract we had. He told me that they couldn't find their copy of what had been in effect. I was asked to come to their office with a copy of the contract so that they could make sure that they were complying with the terms. I did suspect that what I was being told was not the true story, but I felt comfortable with the way the contract was structured. At that meeting, I got the sense that they were trying to work around some of the agreements that had been made originally. It wasn't long before they began to make up reasons that sales were not reported for certain territories. Everyone on their end began to lie about what was happening.

My feeling was that life is too short to get all hung up in what would turn out to be worse for me than staying with it. I was able to make an arrangement with a competing company and drew several of their customers away. I never lied to them, but I never told them what I was doing either. I still made sure I was very careful in any dealings we had going forward. Trust was totally gone, and our contract eventually ended.

It is this type of experience that causes you to be extra cautious when getting involved with others. You can't become a hermit, but you can do your best to be alert to signs of deception.

Duplicity. This basically is saying one thing and meaning another. During this election season, we see that quite often. Some synonyms from *Merriam-Webster* provide further insight: *crooked, deceptive, dishonest, double-dealing, fast, fraudulent, guileful, rogue, shady, sharp, shifty, and underhanded.* While synonyms are not always exactly the same, some of these spill over into the other terms that I have shared. One that was not part of this list is *double-minded.* This seems a lot like *hypocrisy*, but this is more akin to outright lying, as one of the definitions I found calls it. Hypocrisy is pretending to be better than you are. Duplicity means actually doing something that is less than what you are claiming. Duplicity is seeking to trick or deceive someone. In other words, claiming to be better than you are (hypocrisy) is probably not as bad as actually doing something to deceive someone (duplicity).

My guess is that almost all of us have experienced some of these. They are *potholes* because there can be damage or just annoyance depending on the nature and extent of the situation. The challenge for us is to be able to discern the activity and to try to avoid its effects. Most of the time, being a victim of these is not disastrous. We will move on to some that can be very detrimental to our well-being.

CHAPTER 6
Roadblocks

The previous sections were probably a little nuanced in their presentation of some of the ways we can be deceived. In the last two, we will consider how real damage can be done to people or organizations from deceptive acts. A *roadblock* is usually a procedure used to place a temporary barrier to operations. Unlike some uses, I will spell out some instances where people get seriously sidetracked through the actions of others or of themselves. While these are temporary, for the most part, they can also become permanent stoppages if not dealt with appropriately.

SECRETS

Do you have secrets? Of course, you do. There are things only you and God know—at least, you think so. What you think about, how you feel about people and things, etc., these are things you might share with people or you might not.

If you have friends (I hope you do), you don't tell them everything you feel about them. Most of us are very guilty of withholding those feelings we believe will cause a rift between our friends and us. Go ahead and admit it; you lie sometimes.

Let's say your business has a situation not known by other than you and a few other insiders. I want to be very clear here: there is no good reason for being untruthful. There may be merit, however, in withholding some information that could be damaging to your business if it is not unethical.

One significant case in 1984 involved Union Carbide Corp. (UCC). A chemical leak in its Bhopal, India, plant killed over 20,000 people, and over 120,000 were affected somewhat as well. Union

Carbide was found to be responsible, but they denied responsibility. My recollection is that they were felt to be covering it up and dragged their feet on helping those who were affected. The public relations fallout was tremendous.

Compare that with a situation in 1982 where Tylenol products on retail shelves were tampered with. Some of the products had been contaminated with potassium cyanide, and there were a few deaths. Sales temporarily collapsed, but swift action brought the brand back in a relatively short time. A major recall was undertaken, and tamper-proof "gelcaps" made consumers feel much better about the safety of the product. The company regained 92% of the lost sales due to their quick, decisive action.

The point of this comparison is that Tylenol (Johnson & Johnson) was able to overcome a potential catastrophe while Union Carbide didn't. It was generally considered that the problem was UCC's unwillingness to admit what had happened and address it right away. Their situation was a disaster that didn't get settled until 2010.

The "world" doesn't need to know if it is an internal matter. On the other hand, you might need to recall some products if the potential exists that consumers face some danger. If there is no danger but a product could fail prematurely, you have to weigh your actions against the potential backlash that may occur. Lawsuits may ensue. Your quality may come into question with your current and future customers. I was in the business of selling and installing computers in the early days of the personal computer (PC). Someone once accurately said that the quality control was the customer. True, but the retailer was the one who took the hit in terms of complaints and monetary costs.

Many business owners feel that the viability of their company transcends any possible negative effects of a problem. This is mainly a case of determining whether your secret will be found out. The real question, it seems, is whether you reveal the secret to those who need to know or you just let the chips fall where they may. There are, however, many possible consequences to either choice.

One of the real risks of exposing yourself by revealing your secret is that unintended consequences will occur. That is mainly due to competitors pouncing on the opportunity to do you harm by capitalizing on your problem. Almost all the other effects will generally be positive in the end. I can't tell you that doing the right thing is the most economically expedient choice. I can tell you that you can look at yourself in the mirror in the morning and know you can stand tall in the face of criticism. Criticism will come, to be sure, but it will be a lot easier to handle after making the correct choice. Tylenol is a good example of that.

So what is the result of your keeping your secret? Let's say you can pull off the deception and avoid being found out. Is that what you really want? Maybe you can live with it, but my guess is if you are truly an entrepreneur, you care about the market you are serving. The key word here is *serving*. It is not possible, so far as I can tell, to be a servant of your constituency without having their best interests at heart.

This notion applies whether you are trying to serve and protect your stockholders, your employees, or your customers. Being open and honest with all parties is the best solution. It may not be the correct choice from a business standpoint, but it is the one with the most gratifying results. If you have to sidestep some issues in the course of your business, you may be able to live with the outcome. William Shakespeare said in his play *Macbeth*, "To thine own self be true." It's good advice, and it has the outcome of providing you with the ability to live with yourself. In the end, that is the only human entity that matters.

Friends and customers come and go. They will more likely leave you for reasons you can't control than not. How you deal with the fickle nature of those relationships will largely determine how you reconcile your own issues. Doing the right thing is the only satisfying choice. This is true in personal relationships, but it is also important in business ones.

In the end, you must choose who you are trying to satisfy. As a business owner, you need to satisfy your customers, or they will not want your products/services. Also, you will need to give some level of satisfaction to your employees so that they will remain as loyal as possible and do a good job. Your lenders and suppliers will need to be satisfied as well. That usually means doing a reasonable amount of business with them and paying your bill. Keeping all these in whatever loop is significant is crucial to your success.

You walk a tightrope for sure when you decide how much to share with the parties involved. Share too much, and you may find yourself vanquished by your competitors. Keep too much a secret, and you will expose yourself to major problems when found out— and in most cases, you will be.

How each party responds will differ depending on how high their stake is. Employees need their jobs, suppliers need their outlets, lenders need their money paid back, and customers need to have a reliable source of supply of the products and services they require. Remember the discussion on loyalty. It is not a tree that you can anchor your balloon to. Where alternatives exist, you will be at their mercy. Don't make your job more difficult by keeping things from the ones that matter most to you.

ASSUMICIDE

This is probably not a word that has made its way into your vocabulary, but my guess is that you can probably figure out the gist of it. I got it from an article by Ray Pritchard entitled "Victims of Assumicide: What to Do When You Are Misunderstood." It might be called *the blame game* since it is basically our suspicious nature looking for some way to retaliate when we feel we have been disrespected. This is not a small matter; relationships can be destroyed because the hurt we feel can cause us to conjure up all sorts of incorrect notions about the object of our displeasure. In essence, we are using a minute amount of evidence to create a false impression about someone. This is actually a big deal, it seems to me. Pritchard lists a lot of false statements, and I don't want to just repeat what he has written. Assuming someone is up to something untoward that gets out of hand when we don't have facts to back up what we are alleging about them. This may be assigning certain attitudes to them, suggesting they are sleeping with someone, or considering them to be an alcoholic just because you saw them drinking at some event or in a bar.

If this happens to you, any trust you had in the source will probably go out the window. I had an experience once that seemed a lot like this (mentioned in chapter 4). A friend and I had worked together on some projects, and he helped me get the certification that I needed. A while after all this, he came to me with a scheme to get paid for something he didn't earn from an organization I was a member of. I tried to shake it off, but he wouldn't let it go. When I confronted him in the presence of the rest of the members who were to make any decision about his request, he didn't see my actions as appropriate. He tried to get the Internal Revenue Service (IRS), local and regional newspapers, television/radio stations, and people on Facebook to join him in destroying my character. I can't ascribe motives to his actions, but he must have somehow felt that I had wronged him. The story is much longer, and I am not sure it is completely over at this point. I hope he has seen the error of his ways, but I just don't know.

The real problem with situations like this is that they tend to hang around for a long time. Many people just accept them as fact, and even the ones who could dispel such rumors don't make any effort to do so. Unfortunately, there are a lot of people who get some sort of sick pleasure out of seeing others being brought down. Sadly, if we seek to unravel the mess that this has caused, our efforts may not be effective. Pritchard says that we may find our actions to be questioned, our words may be twisted, and our motives may be challenged if we seek to take on the one who has sought to bring us down.

I will address more of how to respond later, but remember, only love can heal the hurt that these accusations cause. The loss of integrity can cripple a person. We find it very difficult to trust someone who has taken such a cavalier approach to relationships.

CRIMINAL ACTS

If we commit a serious crime, chances are our *roadblock* may be a big one. If someone commits a crime that harms you, the effect may also have some ripple effects. Without a doubt, trust can be permanently lost. The seriousness of the matter will dictate a lot of what the outcome will be.

When I was in college, there was a member of the fraternity I was in who committed a series of rather insignificant *misdeeds*. Each of them, in themselves, wouldn't have been an issue if it hadn't been for the number of incidents that occurred. As *brothers*, we tended to overlook all this, and that ended up being a bigger problem in the end. This person was notorious for taking items like belts, shirts, and other personal items without asking. In a real sense, his taking the items was more of a *borrowing* situation than theft. Sometimes, the victim would have an idea of who had the missing items, and they might even let the man keep them—at least for a while. All this came to a head during registration at the beginning of the semester. In those days, the procedure for registering for classes was not an easy process. It involved meeting certain appointed times and then trying to get into the classes that you needed. Missing out on a certain class could disrupt your entire schedule. That meant going back to the drawing board so that all the different classes would fit into the overall schedule.

Much of that wasn't necessary to share, but I wanted to lay out the scene to help readers understand that this wasn't just an annoyance. What happened was the brother had *borrowed* an alarm clock from another brother, who had set it in order to be on time for his registration. I don't remember if this caused him to lose out on what he needed to get scheduled for, but the lack of concern for his fellow man made the perpetrator a very unwelcome member of our fraternity. A trial was scheduled within the fraternity, but the brother charged left school before the trial could begin. No further action was taken, so far as I know. Trust can be a very fragile thing sometimes.

Earlier, I wrote about gullibility. I have been found to be quite gullible at times. I want to believe people are trustworthy, but many are not. There is such a thing as *crimes of opportunity*. This suggests that a criminal might respond to an open purse, a car running in a driveway, etc. Otherwise, they weren't really looking to commit a crime. If that is the case, we may have a difficult time being alert enough to avoid many situations. It is better, I think, to get to know someone well enough to be able to judge their character. I used to watch a series on the *Investigation Discovery* channel entitled *Evil Lives Here*. I had to stop because many of the stories were really hard to watch. In each episode, the speaker was one who had been the victim of a family member, spouse, or close friend. In most cases, they would tell about their early experiences with the person who had ultimately harmed them. While everything seemed OK, the bridging statement to the ultimate outcome was, "But there were signs."

If a criminal act involves a trial and/or a jail sentence, fine, or whatever, plans can go sideways very quickly. Time, money, and loss of trust are all consequences of the actions that led to the outcome. Such matters can affect the future of many people. If restitution is involved, perhaps some of the sentence can be softened on both sides. Even so, a record of such crimes can inhibit the ability to get a job, open a bank account, or a whole host of other things.

SIN

This is a rather controversial topic since many people seem to have an issue with it. In a Sunday school session once, the leader was trying to get to the point where most religions would have some things to agree on. He started with child sacrifice, saying that everyone could agree that it was wrong. Being the one who finds most things to have two sides, I raised my hand. The exact wording of my comment escapes me, but it had to do with the fact that not only do some *religions* still practice that, but we are seeing infanticide today with some of the rulings that have allowed a baby to be killed outside of the womb. These are obviously in dispute in many circles, but I felt that it illustrated the trouble we have agreeing on what a sin is.

Christian Schwarz, creator of the Natural Church Development (NCD) program, uses the Seven Deadly Sins to show how relationships and community development struggle with these same sins. (Note: the *Deadly Sins* were added to Catholic devotions largely due to John Cassian.) Schwarz's presentation shows how there is an *energy* behind each of the sins. These can be surprising to modern-day Christians who feel like the idea of sin is a relative matter.

Nonetheless, this can be a powerful way of addressing some troubling patterns of behavior. The one that I seized on recently was *anger*. The energy behind it, according to Schwarz, is *justice*. In other words, in seeking justice, we are prone to become angry and try to discredit the party/group that is causing others to become angry. This, in turn, has caused the destruction of statues and the creation of riots in response to feelings of alleged racism on the part of the other side of the matter. We will discuss this more later, but the US is still embroiled in a struggle over it as I am writing this. My guess is that we will continue to see this for years to come.

There isn't space to discuss all this, but it is important to realize that enflamed passions can cause us to sin and develop a great deal of distrust. In today's politically charged environment, we are finding a schism between the two major political parties in the US like I have never seen. Even during the Vietnam War, there were enough people with cooler heads to keep things moving in a positive direction. I'm not seeing that today. We are becoming more and more polarized, and one major party is demanding that their constituents follow the *party line* in a lock-step fashion. Reason seems to have left the room, and anarchy is prevalent in many areas. A lot of money is flowing into the ranks of those causing the disturbance, and we seem to be on the brink of a chaotic time. If this changes before the book gets published, I will rewrite this section. If you find it here, you will know that we have some great challenges ahead as a nation. Many people just don't know who to trust these days.

It's interesting how people seem to want to avoid any consideration of sin. It's so subjective in the minds of many that your *opinion* doesn't really matter to them. The *Playboy philosophy* of the 1960s basically put forth the notion that whatever you wanted to do was OK. We all were the captains of our ships, the masters of our souls. Do you see the effects of this today? I surely do. I hope it was my Christian upbringing that made me recoil at these absurd ideas. A little marijuana, a little alcohol, and it's OK for me to do whatever I want to do.

My sense is that sin is just misunderstood. My late wife used to ask people if they would want something done to them that they just did to someone else. Hey, that's Scriptural, isn't it? Of course, that is not good enough for those who just want to *live and let live*. What I mean by being misunderstood is that we just try to avoid the subject altogether. Most people are like those I grew up with: they don't do anything really bad, and they think that is enough to be saved.

I'm beginning to veer off the pathway, and I want to put everything into perspective. However, it is not appropriate to just overlook what might be one of the most important aspects of our lives. We'll come back to this later, but be thinking about how you might be viewed as you work your way through life.

CHARACTER ASSASSINATION

We see this means of bringing things to a halt all the time, don't we? This is a bit like assumicide in that it overlooks the pain that is inflicted on others when we seek to tear down their reputation. There are many of us who would like our lives to have meant something. The notion of *legacy* has been on my mind for many years. As you see others pass on—especially loved ones—you begin to consider what would be the way that we are remembered when we are gone.

In a real sense, we don't know when our time will be up. Henry David Thoreau is famous for saying, "Most of us live lives of quiet desperation." The struggle we face on a daily basis puts a strain on our relationships and causes us to either *hunker down* or kick our lives into high gear to attempt to make our legacy matter. Why is that? Do you think about it often? I'm thinking that at some point, we realize our mortality and sincerely want our lives to matter. Why else are we here? It's not to just be good. Jesus pretty well put that notion to rest.

Our character must be of the quality that makes people want to even remember you. Of course, if you were a funny person, made a lot of money, or were just nice to other people, it might be said that you had left a good legacy. I asked members of a Sunday school class once if they were concerned about their legacy. My best recollection is that most of them said they were. Then I asked them why that was. Not so many responses. The ones I got were pretty much centered around *character*. So, suppose someone destroyed it along the way. I'm thinking that you don't spend too much time wondering why a person ended up as a *derelict* who was a person of note at one time. Too many times, we just comment on how sad it is that they let themselves end up that way. Have you ever considered the possibility that it really wasn't something that they did? I'm hoping that people will remember me for who I really was rather than what I had been purported to be by someone who chose to seek to destroy my reputation.

Character is developed over time. It is the compilation of our true selves and the things that we have done. We don't have to be great executives, philanthropists, or whatever we give our esteem to. The quietness of our lives sometimes conceals who we really are. Most people don't give us much thought because they are too busy focusing on themselves. Consider what it would be like to have the small amount of who we are taken away from us. What kind of legacy would that be?

CANCEL CULTURE

This is a relatively new phenomenon as it pertains to our being able to trust others. It's a bit hard to put your mind around what *cancel culture* really is. Dictionary.com describes it this way: "the popular practice of withdrawing support for (canceling) public figures and companies after they have done or said something considered objectionable or offensive." *Cancel culture* is generally discussed as being performed on social media in the form of group shaming. It seemed rather silly to me, like a childish desire to punish someone who said something you didn't like. In fact, many who have commented on it have the same impression.

Social media has become the bane of many. As this is being written, Twitter and Facebook are taking flack because of keeping something under wraps. I've had items that I posted refused without much reason for it happening. I have also had the person mentioned earlier write some very mean-spirited and completely false accusations posted about me there. The idea of *canceling* someone is ridiculous on its face. TV shows, subscriptions, and insurance policies get canceled.

What this has to do with trust is that such acts, as seen here, cause us to be walking on eggshells most of the time. The notion that we can so easily dismiss someone seems really bizarre to me. For the past decade and before, I have spent most of my time trying to get people into meaningful relationships with each other. I find this to be another of the attempts by perpetrators to break down anything that helps us learn to live with each other. We seem to draw farther and farther away from each other as each day passes. Withdrawal seems to be the only sanctuary for many. The coronavirus has pushed us more in that direction than anything I have seen in my lifetime.

The good news is that this activity has subsided in the past few months. When I was researching this topic, fewer and fewer of them were much past the summer of 2020. The bad news is that this is just a recent iteration of what has been around since humans began to inhabit the earth. We have become more suspicious and fractious of late, and we have several venues that allow us to share our feelings/ attitudes. Sadly, this toxic atmosphere stands in the way of trusting one another.

In the section on *Assumicide*, I mentioned the person who was attempting to *cancel* the project I got started. It was amazing what was written about me in the local newspaper and Facebook. There were several lists of allegations made to the funding agency as well. I was under a cloud of suspicion for a long time, and there are still a lot of the local people who think I am guilty of something. Actually, what I am guilty of is trusting someone that I thought was working in my best interest. In reality, I was set up so that *canceling* me was the fallback position.

UNETHICAL OR IMMORAL BEHAVIOR

There are several of the items in this category that actually relate to this one. Especially the part about *sin* addresses many ways that this behavior can cause a loss of trust. This is intended to wrap up the section by throwing in miscellaneous instances that can cause major problems in *trust*.

Except for the *criminal acts* item, all those addressed here pertain to some sort of personal attack. Criminal acts could actually be personal, but they can also be something that affects a larger group of people as well. Take the Boston Marathon bombing in 2013. There wasn't a particular person targeted, but three people were killed and hundreds injured—some lost limbs. The impact on the lives of those people and their families was very dramatic, but what does this have to do with trust? Well, many people trusted that security would protect them from such harm. Others who saw the perpetrators set down the bags with the pressure cookers trusted that there was nothing bad going to happen with those bags. After the explosions, people dropped their bags while trying to escape the blasts. Many who saw the bags were further terrorized by the possibility of more bombs being present.

One would think that after September 11, 2001, and other bombings, etc., people would be more sensitive to the possibility that other bad actors are lurking out there. Consider the Las Vegas shooter in 2017. All told, sixty-one people were killed and 867 injured. It's pretty hard to always be on alert to possible evil acts, and there were several people who were complicit in this. Family members, the US Air Force, and others knew that the man was mentally unstable. Surely, they knew that he couldn't be trusted, but many people just don't want to get involved.

Certainly, these were illegal, but they were also immoral. More likely than these instances with regard to unethical or immoral behavior are the ways people act that affect a larger group of people. Suppose a person accepts an assignment to be in charge of a major event. For whatever reason, this person doesn't follow through on their responsibility and causes the event to crater. This doesn't rise to the level of being a *roadblock* in some ways. However, the magnitude of the irresponsibility displayed does. What if a person had sexual relations with a person in a high office (political or otherwise) in order to get a favor done for themselves? This might be benign, but it isn't if the quality of what they provide is either subpar or more expensive.

When I had a home improvement center years ago, the local school district issued *requests for quotes* on various items they needed to purchase. One of the categories was paint, and I responded to the request. For several years, I sent in my quotes without being chosen to supply anything. My guess was that I was overpriced, and so I lowered my price each year. Just about the time I was planning to give up on it, a friend of mine chose to run for mayor. He dropped by my store one day and asked if I knew why I wasn't successful on any of my bids. Unlike my suspicion, he told me that the school people said the paint I was providing was inferior. This infuriated me as I knew my brand had outperformed any others in contention. My friend pointed out that the incumbent was perennially being chosen to supply the paint. He also mentioned that the incumbent was very good friends with the president of the school board. My friend asked if I would go on the record with my feelings about the matter, and I agreed.

Without any warning, the local TV station crew showed up at the store and wanted to do a piece on the situation. It turned out very well. I mentioned that the paint factory was owned by the members of the cooperative, and it produced eighty thousand gallons per day. The mayor was also interviewed, and he pulled out a letter from the state attorney general. The letter stated that he was allowed to sell paint to the school district. When I watched this on TV, my thought was, '*OK, it's legal, but is it ethical?*' A lot of people must have agreed it wasn't; my friend won the election. Sadly, nothing changed in the long run. Since the school board president was still the same, the mayor still sold his paint to the district. I gave up on trying to sell them paint since it just wasn't worth the effort. It's pretty sad when people who owe their jobs to the taxpayers don't find it necessary to ensure that the *best* products in every way are chosen for purchase.

PSYCHOPATHIC OR SOCIOPATHIC BEHAVIOR

You may be thinking that I am overstepping the bounds of my expertise now. Well, that's up to you, but I can assure you that I have studied this and have been a victim of it as well. Under the heading of *Assumicide* in this chapter and elsewhere in this book, I have referred to an individual who tried very hard to undo the funding for a grant that he helped me secure. Most of what I have written has to do with his actions and attacks. Just so you know that I know what I am talking about, I am here going to wrap some of it together so that it should be quite plain.

According to Webmd.com, in an article by Kara Mayer Robinson entitled "Sociopath v. Psychopath: What's the Difference" (August 24, 2014), most dictionaries and physicians don't refer to these two conditions by these names. Rather, they call them antisocial personality disorder. I once had a class in graduate school on *organizational behavior*. The instructor said there was no such thing as *personality*. I challenged him on that, and he just made some flip response. I thought he was off his gourd and worked hard to avoid him dinging me for my impertinence. On the other hand, I feel vindicated now because you can't have a disorder for something that doesn't exist. Forgive me for that *detour*, but I couldn't resist it.

The main difference, according to L. Michael Thomkins, EdD, a psychologist at Sacramento County Mental Health Treatment Facility, is the lack of a *conscience* that a psychopath exhibits. A psychopath might steal your money and have no qualms about it, although they might try to hide it. A sociopath might do the same thing but feel badly about it, although it won't stop their behavior.

Neither of the two has empathy (the ability to *stand in other peoples' shoes*), but a psychopath tends to use other people as objects to get what they want. Psychopaths tend to be coldhearted, manipulative, and aggressive in their attempts to get what they want. On the other hand, sociopaths are hotheaded, not caring about anyone except themselves, and they often blame others for what they do. Unlike the portrayal in movies, neither has a propensity for violent behavior. The coldheartedness of psychopaths, however, makes them quite dangerous if they do resort to it.

When I read articles like this during the events leading up to the termination of the project, I became convinced that the behavior of the person involved was indeed *psychopathic*. Certainly, I am no expert, but he was the calmest and most calculating individual I have seen to have been acting as he did in the matter. He didn't exhibit any feelings toward anyone else, and he didn't seem to have a conscience at all. He apparently spent all his time trying to set me up so that he could use me to get what he wanted.

Unfortunately, things happen to us that we can't do anything about.

CHAPTER 7
Breakdowns

It's just my nature.
—Animal fable

The quote above is from a story about a scorpion and a frog. It seems that the frog was sitting on a river bank when a scorpion came along. The scorpion asked the frog to give him a ride across the river. The frog was taken aback at the scorpion's boldness. The frog said he knew that scorpions killed frogs, so he wouldn't do it. The scorpion replied that the frog had nothing to worry about. He said that he would be on the frog's back and would drown if he killed the frog. The frog thought about it a while and then agreed to do it. About halfway across the river, the scorpion stung the frog. As they were bobbing up for the last time, the frog asked the scorpion why he would do that. The reply was, "It's just my nature."

Whether *breakdowns* destroy us or not, they do have a major impact on our ability to function in a normal manner. They aren't just barriers to progress; they are setbacks. Most of us have them at one time or another. If you have, you know how devastating such events can be. In addition to the problem with the event itself, we take a big hit to our willingness to be trusting of many things.

Some of these situations have to do with financial matters, and sometimes, we view them as separate from personal ones. It has been my experience that we eventually find our financial woes to be very personal. Marriages can break up, health issues may develop, and murders or suicides may result. Much of what we see in movies, in one way or another, centers around business and/or finances.

BROKEN RELATIONSHIPS

My first book, *The Dignity of Profit*, had a lot to do with relationships. The title may not truly reveal the full extent of its con- tent. The primary focus was on *community development*. My contention is communities don't form in a meaningful way without relationships. Although a lot of people find a way to avoid it, we are built for relating to one another. A community is made up of various personalities and temperaments. If we try to form groups who don't take other people's gifts and inclinations into consideration, we risk being too one-sided. If that happens, we risk not being able to have successful outcomes.

So even if we do have a relationship that works, maintaining trust is essential to the strong bonds that should be a part of it. If the relationship does not remain sensitive to the fragile bonds holding it together, even seemingly small disagreements can cause a major rift. If you are familiar with the fairy tale *The Princess and the Pea*, you will remember all the efforts to make the princess comfortable. Some feel that her nobility was revealed by her seeking the height of comfort. Most people saw her as a spoiled young woman who couldn't be pleased. I once dated a woman who was very hard to please. It seems she considered herself to be royalty.

It seems important to be flexible in dealing with those you have a relationship. If you can't be accommodating, you will devolve into a state that can easily be *broken*. It is entirely possible trust is at the root of the breach. You may feel that this is a bit of a stretch, but even seemingly unrelated issues can be traced back to a lack of trust. My late wife and I got along pretty well most of the time, but sometimes, I would say something in the presence of others she perceived to be a criticism. She had experienced unwarranted criticism from people growing up. She felt that the trust she had placed in me should have made me realize she wouldn't like me doing that to her. I would profusely apologize, time after time, only to slip up and do it again. It didn't matter that I never intended to say anything to even remotely offend her. In her mind, she didn't feel she could trust me in public because of my lapses of consideration.

Thankfully, we stayed devoted to each other to the end, but there were some times of serious groveling on my part. I would promise to *try* to do better, but she never thought it was enough. She was right, of course. She forgave me, and eventually, I learned to just keep my mouth shut. I'm sure my slips were responsible for other breaches, but I may never know for sure. Let's consider how this might work in other situations.

As a manufacturer's representative as well as a manufacturer, there are some very tenuous connections when it comes to proper representation of a company's products. The principal must have faith in the salesperson's integrity and their allegiance to them. Since the rep doesn't just work for one principal, they risk not being loyal enough to each principal. On the other hand, the rep needs to be able to trust the principal to be loyal to them as well. Setting up other reps in the same territory or selling directly to customers in their territory can cause reps to get very upset. There are more ways that such relationships can be undone. The effect can be very costly to either or both of the parties.

DIVORCE AND ADULTERY

This can be the most personal of all trust breakdowns. When a couple is married, the vows are made at the ceremony, and they include important things having to do with loving and cherishing. While the word *trust* is not necessarily mentioned, it is implicit in the entirety of the vows. For instance, the matter of being rich or poor suggests the couple is saying they can be trusted to stay in the marriage regardless of how tough things get. I'm not sure that marriages are honoring that part too much these days. In the past, marriage had more meaning than it seems to at this point in our history.

Don't get me wrong, there are certainly marriages involving the couple staying together for the *sake of the children* or whatever other reason seems to make sense to them. However, if the arrangement means there is adultery or that love is not a part of it; it should be listed under the category above listed as a *sham*.

Pastor and author Chuck Swindoll said, "Perhaps the best witness we can give as a Christian is to have a reasonably good marriage." When I first heard that, I thought it was a weak, fallback position. Later, I came to realize that the divorce rate among Christians is as high as the general population. Faith is very important to Christians, and it involves having a trusting relationship. Divorce is, for the most part, a breach of trust. My feeling is that anyone who is guilty of that breach cannot be trusted in other things. I may be in the minority, but if one is willing to destroy the most intimate of relationships, how can one be trusted in matters of less importance?

LOSS OF A JOB

The number of people who are devastated by the loss of a job is much smaller than it once was. Nicholas Eberstadt, in his book *Men Without Work* told about there being ten million able-bodied men of working age who didn't have jobs and didn't want to work. Of course, they are probably flying under the radar and not reporting income that they have from various sources. Some of these are men who claim they can do anything, but they can't find a way to finish a job.

There are lots of people who get onto some sort of government assistance and don't really have to work. In fact, if they do work, they are restricted to a relatively small amount of income. Otherwise, they have to pay some of it back. We have a real dichotomy with people wanting to work and not being able to earn over a certain amount. I've known a lot of people who are in such situations. Most of them just go with the flow and take what they are given. Others pick up a little extra here and there, but they don't report it. However, there is a real *cash economy* in many areas. This means a lot of money flowing between businesses and customers never make it onto the tax books. Some get caught, but most don't. There are a lot of them who get away with it because it's not worth the time and effort for the tax folks. When I was building a house in a rural area, one of the workers told me St. Louis people were stupid. What he meant was we didn't know how to get work done for a lower cost by not reporting it for taxes.

I suppose, in some respects, we should applaud these folks for their creativity. However, that is not what it really is—it's skirting the system to their advantage. Don't get me wrong, I certainly want every able-bodied soul who can work to do so. If the job is fulfilling, it can be a boost to a person's ego. So, are we saying that *job loss* is not really a breakdown? Not to my way of thinking. Since the system doesn't function the way it is intended to anyway, the impact on the individual who loses a job may be minimal. Doesn't it seem reasonable to consider that the broken system can take over a person's psyche to the point they just don't care anymore? President Donald Trump helped get people back to work, and the US economy was better off for it. It wasn't just more money flowing, although that did happen. It mainly meant that employers could expand their revenue base because they could produce more in order to reach more markets.

Along comes the coronavirus. Now, the shortfall in the needed expansion in the workforce suddenly made a U-turn. People weren't able to work because the virus was causing businesses to shut down, schools were closed for fear of mass infections, travel was severely reduced, and most people were left with little that could be done about it in the near term. All this made for a major dip in productivity since a lot of the people had to stay away from their jobs. With the confusion about how to get schools and businesses running again, families had a particular problem with how to behave in this new environment.

It is not clear at this juncture whether our economy will ever be the same again. The stock market is tracking very well, but it's not clear whether that is a sustainable situation. We are in uncharted territory, and the presidential election brought in new issues. As of yet, there is no solid plan for how we make our way forward in this new world ahead. As an entrepreneur, I realize that there are some who are flexible enough to change with the times. It's not an unusual scenario for many who depend on the government, but is that sustainable? In areas with *transfer payments* (money that flows from some program into the hands of the needy), there hasn't been as big an impact on the local economy as it is in urban areas. My concern in times like this is that the capital base in many areas can't stand much of hits. On the other hand, these may become attractive to people who have been displaced voluntarily or involuntarily. The American people have been resilient in the past, so we'll see.

This has been a bit meandering, but that is because job loss is not the only issue in our economy at this point. There are so many areas where the situation is just not very stable. Instead of things showing signs of improvement, more things come along to complicate matters. In and of themselves, these are really just annoyances in better times. However, we have not had so many happen at the same time and with the same impact. At some point, we will need to trust somebody or something that is going to be a major factor in how we live in these new times.

BUSINESS FAILURE

This section follows the previous one for some obvious reasons. *Business failure* can be catastrophic at any point because, in a sense, it doesn't matter how it happens. A friend once shared a quote that said, "When you are underwater, it doesn't matter how deep the water is." I'm not sure I buy that completely unless the end is inevitable. There have been many times when I had to recover from some pretty deep water.

Elsewhere, I have mentioned an electrical contracting company that didn't turn out well for me and my partners. When I was a business broker, one of my associates had a listing for the business. I had always wanted to have such a business, and my son-in-law needed to make a career change. The other broker wanted to be involved, and we ended up buying it. As it turned out, the seller required that we keep his brother on the payroll. That made sense since none of us had much of a background in the industry. A combination of sabotage by the brother, our having to pay the *prevailing wage* (union scale) on several jobs, and some unethical moves by a major supplier caused us to have to cease operations. All in all, it was very difficult time for us. We all ended up better off in our future jobs, but it was rather costly for all of us. My son-in-law and I trusted the broker to do the due diligence, and it seems pretty clear that he didn't. Couple that with the nefarious deeds of the seller, and it made for a perfect storm.

As a serial entrepreneur, I have had my share of businesses that didn't turn out the way I wanted them to. How's that for a way to sugarcoat such instances? The point I want to make here is that a cessation of business activity doesn't have to be devastating. I have closed some businesses, but I have also sold some. Each situation was different, and some were pretty hard to swallow. The feeling of loss is more than just no longer having a job. I've come to realize it is a lot easier to get into a business than it is to get out of one. Not only does the sting remain, but so does the financial impact. However, in a real sense, it is similar to a broken relationship. If you started the business, there's a good chance you put a lot more than just money into it. You put a lot of time and a lot of yourself. You have created something that is an innate need in all of us.

According to the IRS and the Social Security Administration, I *retired* over a decade ago. A few years prior to that, my wife and I purchased a sign-making business. A couple of years after that purchase, I went to work for a consulting company. While the latter ended about the time of my *retirement*, the sign shop remains to this day. I also did a few consulting gigs along the way as well. We decided to live our retirement years in a rural setting. OK, I decided, and my wife reluctantly agreed. The original purpose was to build a retreat center to train Christian entrepreneurs. There was an ulterior motive as well: creating a place for our children and grandchildren to visit. Oh, and there was the thing about the cost of housing in the area and the much lower taxes and insurance.

My wife was diagnosed with Alzheimer's disease just about the time we moved into the house we had built on the twenty-three-acre property. That put a crimp in my style, for sure. I had become involved in an organization that was charged with helping to restore tourism and economic activity in an area that had been damaged by a flood. There was a substantial sum with which to operate. I put my work on the retreat center on hold because I didn't have time, money, or the assistance of my wife to get the work done. As I began to become more involved with the economic development project, I came to realize that the board wasn't really geared toward getting much done. My sense still is that they just didn't want to do a lot of work, and there was some concern about friendships possibly causing some stressful decision-making.

My plans for the area began to change dramatically. Through several impactful experiences, I chose to seek funding from the board to rehab some buildings in order to help people start to create new businesses. After receiving some support from various groups, I created a proposal and ultimately received funding to purchase a building to rehab and put the structure in place to make this project a reality. The work was done, and the project is over. It was successful in many respects, but it has turned over to the grantor. The attempts to garner the necessary support from the community were not fruitful. I mentioned earlier some of the other factors that made it less than it could have been.

The reason for sharing all this has to do with the trust factor being a tenuous one at best from the beginning. I was frankly surprised that the project proposal was funded 100 percent. The building was purchased from some people who didn't think it was important to share some of the issues that caused a substantial sum in order to get corrected. Due to the shortfall in initial funding that resulted, much hands-on work had to be done by me and others involved in the project. When things got tough, attrition became another challenge. On top of all that, the person mentioned in Chapter 6, who was originally supposed to be helping obtain funds for the nonprofit venture going forward, turned on me. His plan was to get my project overturned in order to cover his own nonperformance problem with the economic development board. It's a long, sorted story, but we worked through it…for the most part.

Through this, many trusted relationships went by the wayside. In many respects, the perceived lack of trust existing from the beginning turned out to be quite real. What makes this hurt so much is that I stepped forward to attempt what the board didn't want to do. I received no pay for all the work I performed and even spent thousands of dollars to help make up the shortfall that no one else was willing to do. There was very little support from the folks who were to provide it in the beginning. It's a pretty uncomfortable position when you are just out there twisting in the wind. I don't wish that on anyone.

One of the major aspects that also fell by the wayside was my desire to help create a leadership group. There were so many things needed to be done but needed outside support. I speculate often about what the root causes might have been, but there may be too many to actually make any judgments about. In my early days in the area, I met with a couple of the more interested citizens. As I related my reasons for being there, one of them said to me, "If you are successful at getting this done, your fingerprints will be all over the place, but no one will know who you are." My response was that as a consultant, I had to be that way all the time. It's pretty rare that a client pushes the consultant out front as the one who saved their business. I actually did have it happen once, and I was mentioned in a national magazine. Ironically, my principal thought I shouldn't have let them do it—like I had anything to do with it.

As this has turned out, my fingerprints are all over, but my name has been mentioned often. Unfortunately for everyone, I have become somewhat of a villain to those who don't know the real story. The people who do know it chose not to get involved in the matter. I just find it harder and harder to stomach the lack of trust that seems to come from every direction.

I once facilitated (led) an online course on *Business Ethics* for Indiana Wesleyan University. It had a more positive focus than I expected. However, the students were pretty hard on some of the cases that were presented. None of them had a business background, so they were looking at things from the perspective of consumers.

There is a balance that has to be met when handling any transaction. If someone is on the short end of the stick, the balance will not be maintained. While it is extremely important in many cases to be wary of others, we have to find a way to get along, or life will be tough for us.

The next section is about overcoming these obstacles. That's not always possible, but we must make the effort. In many cases, we must just walk away. How we work through the challenges that these considerations demand will determine our path to a more rewarding and less stressful life.

PART III

WHAT TO DO WHEN TRUST IS LOST

The farther you go down the list in Part II, the harder it is to get past the breach that has been created with the loss of trust. The closer you are to the person or group who has harmed you, the harder it is to rebuild trust. For instance, if it is a family member or church group, you would naturally expect there to be trust. Obviously, that is not always the case. As an only child, I was shielded a lot because I had no issue with my parents or grandparents. On the other hand, the same couldn't be said for some who got more distant. It's relatively easy to stay away from many of them anyway.

If you cannot remove yourself from people who have betrayed the trust you had, you may want to try to repair the broken relationship. That's where we are going next—what can be done to get past the obstacles that have been put in your path.

CHAPTER 8
Overcoming Obstacles to Trusting

In a real sense, we have a major role in being able to trust others. By that, I mean we have to be comfortable enough with a relationship to either overlook the shortcomings of others or try to find common ground upon which to work things out. If we can't accomplish any of these, we probably should just move on. US Supreme Court Justice Clarence Thomas was put under a heavy burden to prove that he was not guilty of the allegations of Anita Hill. Justice Thomas made a statement during the hearing that it is hard to prove a negative. That is, to prove that you didn't do something. There have been many instances since then with regard to nominees to the court that were alleged to have done something that ultimately was not proven. However, it really challenges the notion that we are innocent until proven guilty.

One of the stories written earlier had to do with my being accused of preventing a person from earning a fee that he actually hadn't earned. Item after item was presented that had no basis in fact. The outcome so far has been that some people feel I was guilty of the charges and accepted these allegations out of hand. Nothing has ever been taken up in the legal system because there hasn't been anyone who was willing to take the case on. Personally, I wanted to refute his charges in the same arena that he had presented his. My board of directors talked me out of it, and the attorney we consulted felt that damages would be hard to prove. Clearly, extortion was his game.

The process was costly to me personally in terms of reputation and out-of-pocket costs. Over a year later, nothing has come of it, but who knows if it is really over? A major breach of trust had occurred during this process, and it will probably never be restored. I felt the same way after I sued my former partner and the bank that had made the loan for our business. My attorneys felt that I had been unfairly treated, but they weren't willing to make the appeal on a contingency basis. In that case, almost everyone in the small Mississippi city felt that I had been wronged, but that didn't help with the pain of being unable to complete the dream I had for the business we were operating. The lawyers tried to console me, but in the end, they had to admit that nothing good seemed to have come out of it for me. A lot of trust was lost in that instance, and I already knew I wouldn't do it again.

So, is this what we are left with? We may or may not have anything redeeming to come out of a bad situation. Frankly, I hope not, but I also am not willing to accept that as a reasonable outcome. Life is not fair in some ways, but *zero-sum* outcomes don't have to be that way. Is it always just one way or the other? As an entrepreneur, I have refused to declare something as dead until all hope is exhausted in trying to save it. Clearly, there are situations where we have to stop trying, but we should be satisfied that we have done all we can to save it. Perseverance can pay off in a lot of ways that may not seem plausible to many.

CONNECTING OBSTACLES TO MOTIVES

As I mentioned before, people have motives for doing what they do. Sometimes, they may not be conscious of them, but they are there nonetheless. In Chapter 6, I shared information about the Seven Deadly Sins. The one that I focused on was *anger*. We will deal with that one separately as it has a very prominent role in our attitude toward trusting others.

So here is a brief overview of possible connections to the *obstacles in the previous chapters:*

- *Poor Directions. Sloth* may fit this obstacle as it is a lack of caring: *My attitude is I couldn't care less about what you want.*
- *Detours.* Perhaps *envy* could be a motive here: *I would rather be doing what you are.*
- *Potholes. Lust* can be the root of this: *I use others to get what I want.*
- *Roadblocks.* The actions here suggest that *greed* could be the motive: *I don't want to have to give up what I have.*
- *Breakdowns. Pride*, the over-arching sin behind all the Seven, causes us to seek what we want over the needs and desires of others.

Anger was mentioned in several places, and there's more about it in the section entitled "Dealing with Anger Issues" coming up. *Jealousy*, while not one of the list of deadly sins, is quite damaging, as I pointed out. It's pretty easy to see how it impacts the list in many areas.

As we look deeper into the possible causes, some of them will seem to be unworthy of consideration. However, looking back at the possible impact of the obstacles they cause, I'm not sure that anything that lacks love and concern for our fellow humans can be dismissed. In the case of my fraternity brother, who *borrowed* things, the outcome was just delayed until it reached the point of being a problem. We may be OK for a friend to take a belt of ours without asking, but it is highly inconsiderate, at the least.

In a real sense, anything that impacts *relationships* will ultimately affect the community at large. Each of us owes consideration of, if not allegiance to, what helps build a strong sense of belonging. In my two previous books, the main focus was always about community. Without relationships, we may find it very difficult to make a community strong—if we can have it at all.

The next section is a deeper look at what may be going on when obstacles arise.

FLUSH OUT THE ROOT CAUSES OF THEIR MOTIVES

Unless we are the *fight-or-flight* kind of person who just reacts instinctively, we should be able to take a deep breath and reflect. Then, we should be able to begin to look at what is at the heart of the matter. We need to try to find what motivates the other people. Attempt to sort through the various issues that appear to be driving their actions. I'm not a psychologist, but I believe that people don't do things for no reason. Some are more basic than others, but we all still act out of one or more categories.

Here are some reasons why people are untrustworthy. Interestingly, it seems these are also the same types of things that cause people to have difficulty trusting people:

1. There have been one or more instances where the person has not been responsible in smaller matters. Therefore, they can't be trusted in other things, especially bigger things. Jesus

told a parable about three men who were given money to do something with. One of them didn't perform. The answer Jesus gave as to why this mattered was that there wasn't trust enough to give the man greater responsibility. Albert Einstein said, "Whoever is careless with the truth in small matters cannot be trusted with important matters."

2. In today's culture, we see a lot of people who are so self-absorbed that they can't even fathom the need to care about others. This shows up in almost every situation we are involved in. A psychological personality disorder known as *narcissism* is an extreme instance of this. There are too many symptoms to get into here. The irony of this is that their high esteem may actually be hiding a sense of inadequacy. One of the more significant problems with this is that they may be manipulative. This makes them very untrustworthy because they are seeking to do whatever makes them look better.

3. *Gaslighting* seems to be a rather new phenomenon. It is an attempt to discredit a person by calling into question something that is part of their history. This is a sign of a person who is abusive and may be trying to create mental problems for others.

4. The person may come from an environment of untrustworthiness. If lying and conniving are part of their upbringing, they may feel that it is required to be successful. In such cases, anything allowed in that environment is fair game for them now.

5. *Laziness* may be the cause of people promising to do something and then not doing it. They may not see the benefit of following through on what they had agreed to. It may also be that the consequences of not doing what they had agreed to do were just not severe enough to compel them to do it.

6. *Forgetfulness* may be understandable, but that doesn't make it acceptable. If the person has a disorder, they are just not a candidate for what you need them to do.

7. If a person is an *outright crook*, the answer is easy. It is not up to us to try to change them. However, sometimes people get backed into a corner and feel they just don't have any choice but to do whatever is best for their survival. An example is folks who are displaced from their homes during a hurricane, a tornado, or the like. Looting is not a good thing, and there are many who are just taking advantage of a bad situation.

However, getting food or supplies needed to survive can surely be forgiven.

8. *Tribalism* can trigger people to behave in ways that would normally be contrary to their character. I addressed this in *The Dignity of Profit* and *The Dignity of Service*. This is also discussed in chapter 2 in the section entitled "Societal Issues—Lack of Concern."

9. *Lack/loss of integrity* essentially creates a major breakdown in the ability to be trustworthy. I have touched on this, and I will have more to say about it later. The reason is having integrity is the essence of being trustworthy. The loss of it can mean you forfeit many opportunities and/or lose positions that you are holding.

This list is not exhausting by any means. Most of what is not addressed here is either just an annoyance or has to be dealt with by professionals. In the cases of *poor directions* and *detours*, there is possibly no malicious intent involved. It would be hard to discern it if there is. Beyond that, the other situations can be very damaging to you, your family, or others with whom you have a relationship. You should probably seek professional assistance in dealing with them.

DEAL WITH ANGER ISSUES

You may be wondering what the deal is with this seemingly abrupt change in the text. It's really not, however, as I hope to explain. In the presentation about the Seven Deadly Sins, I also specifically mentioned anger. This is the sin that has *justice* as the negative force. The point made by Christian Schwarz, NCD founder, is that anger can have a self-righteous side to it when we choose to take matters into our own hands. God is about justice, and He will deal with it. Our role is to seek *loving relationships*, which is one of the eight Quality Characteristics of the NCD program. It seems that trying to include love in a heated debate might be a little dangerous. When Lyndon Johnson was president, he commented once on the difficulty of trying to extricate the US from the Vietnam War. His take on it was that it is like riding on the back of a raging tiger—you don't know whether it is better to ride it until it gets tired, or try to jump off and risk being killed.

Pastor Chip Ingram points out that anger is a *secondary emotion*. This follows the NCD position that *justice* is the energy that drives anger. As we are disrespected or have instances that we feel are examples of an attempt to deprive us of our rights, we choose to react negatively rather than in a positive manner. In doing so, we ascribe motives to others that may not be accurate. Additionally, we are likely guilty of something that negates our ability to challenge someone else's actions.

The point of bringing this up is to illustrate the challenge of getting to the heart of trusting others. I've known a lot of people, many of them from racial minorities, who just don't want to be appeased. I can't blame them for that, but there are other solutions that can work. Unlike some of the other obstacles, there should be some folks who truly want to make progress on the issues they face. Part of the problem, it seems, is that there are others who don't want there to be progress. There is such a lack of trust that solutions don't seem to be the object of the struggle. Feelings run deep, and this issue has been around for a long time. The insincerity on both sides of the argument is palpable. Trust demands that empathy be a part of the dialog.

SHOW CONCERN

In the last sentence of the previous section was the mention of the need for empathy. According to greatergood.berkeley.edu, it is defined as "the ability to sense other people's emotions, coupled with the ability to imagine what someone else might be thinking or feeling." It is sort of like *walking a mile in someone else's moccasins*. Concern might also be through *sympathy*, but that doesn't have the deeper meaning that empathy conveys.

One of my favorite sayings is, "People don't care how much you know until they know how much you care." I don't know who to credit for it, but it nails the notion of being sensitive to other's needs. This is not to say that we just go over to their side. If we are dealing with untrustworthy people, they need to hear the truth, not sympathy. The matter of concern also addresses *tough love* that can truly make a difference in many situations.

For many years, I have been a student of negotiation, and I have been involved in several myself. Most people don't really understand the nuances of negotiating and consequently don't do very well at it. Although limited, my success has come when I have taken the time and effort to learn what is going on in matters of trust. In order to be able to gain the confidence of the parties involved, one must learn what they can about them. This is a great trust builder and can be the way to tip the scales in the right direction. Having a neutral party handle the negotiations can go a long way toward a satisfactory solution.

LOOK FOR OPPORTUNITIES TO REBUILD TRUST IN SMALL WAYS

Samuel Johnson once wrote, "It is better to suffer wrong than to do it, and happier to be sometimes cheated than not to trust." To this point, we have discussed the obstacles and how to begin the process of rebuilding trust. There is no cookie-cutter approach to getting that done. It is indeed a process, and we will tackle the likelihood of being successful in the next chapter. For now, I want to address moving past the empathy step. It is time now to become committed to getting the real work done. There is no assurance that we will achieve our goals, but having a strong commitment to engage in the hard work is where we need to begin in earnest. We need to have realistic expectations, or we will not make it out of the gate.

Booker T. Washington, an American educator and reformer who rose from slavery to found what is known as Tuskegee University, wrote, "Few things can help an individual more than to place responsibility on him, and to let him know that you trust him." Giving people the opportunity to redeem themselves is a powerful step in the right direction. It doesn't have to be a major move; it just needs to be a positive one. Expectations must be set, and desired outcomes should be clear. Any necessary training should be done if this is a work or organizational setting. Regular checks should made in order to ensure that the process is working as it should.

Now, I'm not an expert in this, but anyone can come up with what they feel is appropriate insofar as trusting is concerned. We have looked at this earlier, and hopefully, you have begun to formulate a plan to deal with this on your own. If you have to have a mediator, you need to decide if it's worth all that. After all, there are limits to what a person should do to help someone become trustworthy. What I have found to be the most important initial step is to be intentional about it. The more we can be trusting, the more pleasant and productive life can be. It is, however, a process, and it takes effort and determination.

FOCUS ON POSSIBILITIES FOR SUCCESS

In order to be able to do what has been proposed above, there need to be opportunities to be able to learn and grow from mistakes and failures. As we will address in the next chapter, it takes a much longer time to rebuild trust than to achieve it in the first place. There will be fits and starts involved, but each setback should be a chance to experience what building trust is like. Each opportunity should offer greater responsibility to strengthen the relationship that should be developing through the process.

In *The Dignity of Profit*, I wrote about defining success. Yogi Berra once said, "If you don't know where you are going, how will you know when you get there?" Of course, *trust* is the goal, but you have to have a picture of what that looks like. In the earlier chapter, I wrote about what it means to trust someone. It's a subjective matter in some ways. Each of us knows what we believe trust to be. If it is not clear, *how do we know when we get there?* The fact that our view of trust might be subjective doesn't have to be negative. As long as our motives are honorable, we should be able to articulate what we expect.

Working together to determine how to succeed at rebuilding trust is extremely important. It should take the appropriate time and should be a sober activity. By this, I mean that it should be approached very seriously. After all, the process of rebuilding is going to be difficult. Without total agreement, we can be wandering in the dark and not know whether we are really achieving anything. This is too important to be treated lightly.

In Neil Rackham's book *S.P.I.N. Selling*, we are introduced to the acrostic shown in the title. The full name of the process he advocates is Situation – Problem – Implications – Needs payoff. If we go through the first three without having a real *payoff*, we will have done what my Air Force flight instructor referred to as *practice bleeding*. I don't know about you, but this never seemed like a good idea to me. The goal is to restore trust if at all possible, and we need to stay focused on where that is going to take us.

CHAPTER 9
Is It Really Possible to Restore Trust?

Up to this point, we have been identifying areas that lead to mistrusting others, considering what may be behind their actions, and looking for ways to help identify the root causes. We now come to the place where we have to determine if it is really possible to overcome those issues and restore trust. Thomas J. Watson (IBM CEO who guided the company into great success) once said, "The toughest thing about the power of trust is that it's very difficult to build and very easy to destroy." If you have had an experience with the loss of trust, you know this statement to be true. Further, the more you have instances of betrayal, the harder it is for you to be trusting at all.

THE CHALLENGE OF RESTORING TRUST

Author Stephen Covey said, "The ability to establish, grow, extend, and restore trust is the key professional and personal competency of our time." Each of us has a background that includes many experiences that affect our ability to trust. Our personalities are formed by our culture, the role models in our lives, nurturing (or lack thereof), our values, self-awareness, and emotional maturity. These form our *paradigm*, which provides the filter through which input is measured. This is very personal and probably is not like anyone else's. It's been interesting to me to engage others who have different backgrounds from mine.

The more you find in common with others, the more you are willing to trust. You can compare notes, so to speak, and that forms bonds that may lead to relationships. On the other hand, these may not be the best relationships. Many times, we find ourselves being mistreated in some way by other people. In such cases, it is easy to begin to feel that there isn't anyone who really cares about your situation. Then you come in contact with someone who has had a similar experience as yours. If it is for real, you tend to bond, and you are leaning on each other for support. While it is true that the world seems to be against you, it may be that your approach is to become so connected that you withdraw. There are cases where withdrawal is an appropriate response. Sometimes, it means that you become so inwardly focused that you just don't connect with the *outside world*. This will cause you to miss a lot of what life is all about, and it might set you up for a crash if one of you decides that this is not what you want.

Now, I am not a psychologist, and I didn't play one on TV or stay at a Holiday Inn Express last night. I do, however, have a lot of experience with relationships. Most of them were business or organizational ones where there are presumably common goals. Even then, egos can get in the way. If you are familiar with the book/movie entitled *Cheaper by the Dozen*, you may remember that the father of this tribe was an *efficiency expert*. I read that book as a requirement when I was in elementary school, I think. This is my nature, and I just don't do well in settings where there are people who blather on and take an inordinate amount of time that is not productive. That makes relationships difficult for me.

In a psychologytoday.com article entitled "Great Relationships Require Hard Work, But Not Forever," Linda and Charlie Bloom shared some thoughts on relationship building: "The required effort is often great, and the challenge can be daunting, leading many to conclude that it's not worth it or that they don't have the stamina and perseverance to work forever at this level." This article was written mainly about couples, but there are some applications for any situation. The point, for me, is that an initial reason for becoming *related* may become less of a connection over time. We are in a political season, and the differences between many of the candidates are stark. If you find yourself in a group that supports a particular candidate, you might have an intense connection to some in that group. Once the election is over, the rest of the attributes of the respective parties may not really draw you into a long-lasting relationship. If one of you has a desire to remain in a relationship and others don't, the consequences could cause that person to devolve into a lower state than before the relationship began.

I don't think that it is a great leap to say that any relationship requires that *common bond* I wrote of above. If it is something that is transitory, like a political contest, the end of the bond may spell the end of the relationship, but it doesn't have to. I've moved a lot due to business changes, etc. In each case, my wife and I looked for a church that seemed to fit our needs. Yes, we did consider ourselves to be *needy* in that way. However, we weren't looking to create relationships; those came when the connection was right. In fact, we still maintain them, in many cases, long after we no longer have direct contact with them. My wife and I were very close, and we didn't *need* others to make it work.

The Blooms went on to write, "We tend to think that if the *feeling* is there, then the relationship should just 'naturally' thrive." You may know that *feelings* can be deceptive, and they can be fleeting. In order for a relationship to live on, there needs to be a core. This word is derived from the French word *coeur*. The basic meaning of that word is "*heart*." Jesus said, "For where your treasure is, there will your heart be also" (Matt. 6:21, NIV). What do you treasure? If it is material things like a Jeep, perhaps you might join a club for Jeep owners. Now, that is certainly something that might feed your passion for banging around in rough terrain. On the other hand, you may or may not have anything else in common with others in the club.

SOMETHING NEEDS TO CHANGE

So, what in the world does all this have to do with restoring trust? The most enduring relationships are built on trust. The deeper the bonds in those relationships, the stronger the trust becomes. Consequently, a breach of trust can sometimes be overcome, but it may not be irrevocable. In a marriage, sexual infidelity may not be overcome. In many ways, if it happens, trust in the offender may have been misplaced in the beginning. Forgiveness is important, but we humans have a tough time with forgetting. My wife and I had a very strong bond, but thankfully, I never had to decide if I could overcome the commission of an act of infidelity like that. It was never a matter of consideration for either of us.

There has to be some basis upon which to make a restoration, or there just may not be a way to *right the ship*. Since I never had to forgive what I consider the most egregious of sins in a marriage, it is hard for me to comment on this. What I can do is to help provide some positive insights in avoiding breach in the first place. This may seem like a cop-out, but I believe therapeutic information should be the province of those best equipped to provide it. My recommendation would be to seek a good Christian counselor for such matters. Those folks can deal with heart issues much better than secular ones. The point is that we need to determine the best outcomes in these cases, and my *trust* is in those who have a higher calling. Some readers will take issue with this, but my experience comes from some training in both worlds. To that point, the solutions that I have seen from secular sources just can't measure up to those who have an eye on the eternal.

So, we get to the obvious point that a one-sided breach means that there has to be a change in behavior. An attitude of forgiveness on the part of the offended one doesn't mean that the relationship can continue. We are called to forgive as Christians, but with trust being the overpowering issue, it's just really hard to overcome the pain of infidelity. Unfortunately, many relationships just don't weather the storms that are present in such cases. There are actually some nonsexual situations, but they are not considered as *infidelity*. For my part, I consider a breach of trust akin to infidelity in many ways. We're going to look at that in the next section.

RELATIONSHIPS VS. TRANSACTIONAL INVOLVEMENT

Since we have been mainly looking at relationships as intimate rather than just transactional, it seems important to consider the connection between the two. I have provided a good bit of information regarding relationships and the loss of trust. Transactions, to me, are a matter of sales: a seller offers, and a buyer purchases. You may wonder just what this has to do with trust. There is actually a relational connection between a buyer and a seller. The seller is offering a product or service at a price, and the buyer gives the seller something of value in return. Implicit in these exchanges is *understanding* that the seller has been forthright in any claims, and the buyer is accepting the claims to be valid.

Certainly, this has implicit in it that not every transaction involves a relationship. If you go to a business that sells something that the buyer picks out, there may not be any responsibility on the part of the seller. An example would be a gravel pile where the quality is not an issue. If the buyer finds what he/she wants, they get what they pay for, and nothing else is involved. On the other hand, if there is a quality issue involved in the transaction, getting what you paid for makes it more personal. I have that happen, and a refund is in order.

As-is transactions can get a bit thorny as well. In real estate sales, most sales are done on an *as-is* basis. However, if the seller knows of or should have known of a problem, they have an obligation to disclose anything that constitutes a structural matter. While there should be a trust factor, contracts can help to avoid issues in that regard. I find it amazing just what extent sellers can go to try to skirt the problems that exist in a property they are offering for sale. It is unfortunate that the purchase of a personal dwelling can be so fraught with unethical or even illegal attempts to deceive. Individual sales usually don't have a relational component since the buyer may never meet the seller. In such cases, any agency *relationship* makes the difference as to whether there is a *clean deal* or not. I've had some very unpleasant experiences with realtors, but not ones who were representing my property or interest.

According to Oxford University Press online, the definition of *agency* is "a business or organization established to provide a particular service, typically one that involves organizing transactions between two other parties." While *relationship* is not specifically included in this definition, it is what makes an agency responsible for taking care of its clients' best interests. Otherwise, it would not be necessary to pay for assistance that you are not getting. So here is where relationships and transactions come together.

The point in all this is that most transactions do involve some level of relationship. Therefore, there is a level of trust that is expected in them. While contracts are a part of many transactions, they don't cover everything that is done. On the other hand, having someone make sure that everything is taken care of provides a great deal of comfort to most of us. Without trust giving you that comfort, you may be disappointed and even suffer financially in the transaction.

Frankly, we are on our own in most of our transactions—retail stores, vehicle purchases and repairs, utility hook-ups, etc. This gets us back to the chapter on the importance of trust in our lives. The sad part about this situation is most of us just don't have time to deal with all the transactions that go on. We place an order for something online, pay with a credit card or electronic check, and trust that nothing bad is going to happen. However, the reality is there are so many things that could go wrong; we could be freaked out most of our time worrying when and how it is going to happen.

WHAT HAPPENS IF THIS DOESN'T WORK

Since there are so many opportunities for things to go wrong, the chances of a catastrophic event happening are actually pretty high. I hope you aren't thinking I would just dump all this on you and leave it there. Certainly not, but there aren't any clear-cut answers to avoiding the loss of trust. For that matter, there aren't many good ways of restoring trust either. On the other hand, learning to discern can be a very helpful way to keep yourself out of most problems. If you can do it, many situations can be avoided in the beginning.

Philosopher Johann Wolfgang von Goethe wrote, "You can easily judge the character of a man by how he treats those who can do nothing for him." We live in a culture that is mostly overcome with *self-love*. Many are so focused on themselves that they don't have the capacity to think of others. In *The Dignity of Profit,* I wrote a good bit about relationships and accountability. It is hard to form relationships with people who are *self-absorbed*. St. Augustine called people that don't care about others as having a *heart turned in on itself*.

None of us is perfect; I hope you realize that. Therefore, we are obliged to recognize our shortcomings and look for ways to connect with others. Building relationships with people you can trust is vital to a well-balanced existence. In the next chapter, we are going to look at how we can become trustworthy ourselves. It we can achieve it for ourselves, it is quite possible we will accomplish two things: (1) we will have a better understanding of what to look for in others, and (2) we have a chance to attract others to ourselves who are looking for the authenticity and character we are reflecting.

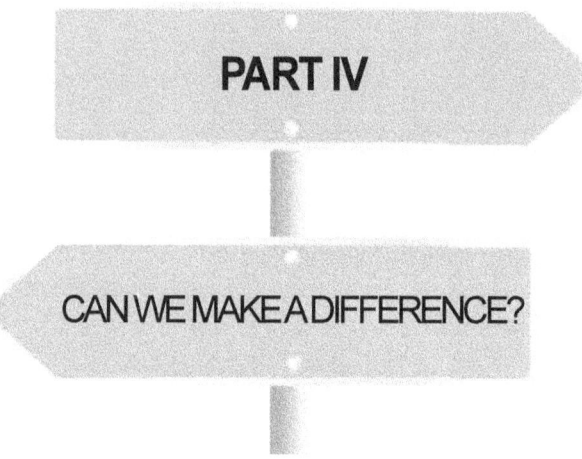

He that takes truth for his guide, and duty for his end, may safely trust to God's providence to lead him aright.

—Blaise Pascal

Blaise Pascal is a very famous person. He lived during the seventeenth century and was a French mathematician, physicist, inventor, philosopher, writer, and Catholic theologian. In Christian theology, he is well-known for what has been called *Pascal's Wager*. Basically, Pascal argued that a rational person should live as though God exists and seek to believe in God. If God does not actually exist, such a person will have only a finite loss, whereas if God does exist, he stands to receive infinite gains and avoid infinite losses.

This has a few problems, including the fact that it is somewhat circular reasoning. There are also other religions making the same claim. Pascal was highly acclaimed, nonetheless, due to some breakthrough thinking on probability theory. The point for us here is we still have a choice as to where to place our trust.

We can also, however, place alongside this theory the notion of everyone having a "God-shaped" hole in our heart that only God can fill. Pascal has also been credited with that theory, although it seems to be a bit less clear. Here's a point to take away from this as we consider being trustworthy: our belief in God opens the door to a lot of possibilities in terms of how to live our lives. Personally, I have many instances I could cite that would seem implausible were there no basis for belief in God. My faith and experience have enabled me to see God's handiwork in great abundance in our world. In many ways, the *Wager* choice was what has made this possible for me. "You will see it when you believe it" is the way the statement goes that gives us a basis for how to make that *leap of faith*.

In a real sense, the notion of *faith* has a lot to do with our ability to *trust*. *Blind faith* may seem preposterous to you, but that could change if you were to adopt a different *belief system*. I have always thought of myself as a rational person, but the notion of blind faith can also fit into my belief system. I'm not philosopher enough to engage in an argument about this. I just happen to have enough faith and experience in order to be able to accept the possibility in certain circumstances. In the end, it has to do with how much trust we are willing to place in the Source.

CHAPTER 10
Is Our Trustworthiness Enough?

> Through it all, through it all, I've learned to trust in Jesus;
> I've learned to trust in God.
>
> —Andraé Crouch

I've sort of danced around the matter of God throughout this book. I have blatantly written about certain matters in that regard. All in all, it is my belief that we don't have a lot of basis for trust outside of the realm of Christianity. God has proven Himself to be trustworthy, and the witnesses and instances abound in the Holy Bible, in extra-Biblical literature, and from very credible sources we can actually interview.

The problem will always lie in the challenge of verifying the sources. Remember the quote from Mortimer J. Adler about there being too many facts? When we consider God as the ultimate source, it immediately becomes challenging to make a clear case without including reason to some extent. It's not like we could put God into any situation where we could question His veracity. On the other hand, the absolute proof required for most arguments is tough to acquire.

At the risk of stepping all over my thoughts in any argument regarding trust, I am going to lay out the case for accepting God as the only true source we have for trustworthiness. If we do that, we can take the steps offered below and be assured of our own ability to be trustworthy.

GOD AS THE SOURCE

Dr. Tony Evans once challenged those who used *resources* as their basis for making proclamations about Christianity. His take on it was that we should go to the *Source* instead. He was referring to God because He is the only true source of our faith. We can use what we have received through prayer, but that is subject to being just your take on what God has provided. The only infallible Source is the Word of God as given to us in the Bible.

I can almost hear the grumbling from those who question the statement I gave. John Wesley cited four sources (Wesleyan Quadrilateral): scripture, tradition, reason, and Christian experience. Scripture was considered the living core of the Christian faith and, therefore, the sole foundational source. The others besides scripture help to support scripture, but they surely can't trump it. *Sola scriptora* (only scripture) is held by other Protestant Christian denominations. They reject any original infallible authority other than the Bible.

However, the percentage of American Protestants who accept *sola scriptora* is less than 50 percent, but it seems that much of that is due to the belief that faith and works are both required for salvation. You may be in the higher percentage who believes otherwise, but that doesn't make it correct. I find those who believe in the infallibility of the Scripture to have a compelling argument, and I, therefore, support that position. I'm just not sure that questioning the scripture helps provide clarity to what our faith is all about. My *experience* as a Christian certainly squares with scripture.

Since I have come to know God in many of His wonderful ways, I find great comfort in the faith I have that He is not capricious (whimsical). I'm not sure how we are supposed to navigate through life without the sense of there being an anchor we can hold to. Experiences I have provided in this book are only a few instances of how God has been with me on my journey. While I don't always understand His ways, I have faith in His caring for me. He is my guide and my strength, and in that, I find great comfort. Looking back on outcomes, I am amazed at how He works things out. Many others have shared their stories, and each one adds to my strong belief in God's ways.

Here are some scripture passages and quotes that provide comfort. They relate to the Bible, but they have been proven over and over:

God is not a man, so he does not lie. He is not human, so he does not change his mind. Has he ever spoken and failed to act? Has he ever promised and not carried it through?
(Num. 23:19, NLT)

It is not the strength of your faith but the object of your faith that actually saves you.
—Timothy Keller, American pastor, theologian, and Christian apologist

Faith is the gaze of a soul upon a saving God.
—A. W. Tozer, *The Pursuit of God*

Understanding is the reward of faith. Therefore, seek not to understand that you may believe, but believe that you may understand.
—St. Augustine of Hippo

Reason is, in fact, the path to faith, and faith takes over when reason can say no more.
—Thomas Merton, American Trappist monk and theologian

Decide to trust Him for one little thing today, and before you know it, you find out He's so trustworthy you be putting your whole life in His hands.
—Lynn Austin, *Candle in the Darkness*

We must cease striving and trust God to provide what He thinks is best and in whatever time He chooses to make it available. But this kind of trusting doesn't come naturally. It's a spiritual crisis of the will in which we must choose to exercise faith.
—Charles R. Swindoll, American Evangelical pastor

BE A PERSON OF INTEGRITY

If you are reading this book, I hope it means that you consider yourself to be trustworthy. Of course, the other reason is that you want to find ways to trick others or avoid getting caught if you are up to something.

> *Your commitment to honor is tested daily through temptations and seductive opportunities—mostly, no one knows or sees these micro-events of integrity. But what matter? You know, and therein lies the greatest pleasure of honor, your self-respect.*
> —Dr. Laura Schlessinger

On the other hand, this only matters if you are indeed a person of integrity. If you are not, you might just be smug enough to find comfort in being able to agree with yourself. We all have lapses on occasion, so it takes a lot to establish ourselves as having integrity.

Integrity sort of rules the roost when it comes to standards of authenticity. It's been said by many that the *one-way approach* to character is what we are finding in a person of integrity. "Faith is a strong belief in someone or something without logical proof. But, trust is a firm reliance on the character or integrity of another. I've developed a *faith* in God—a belief that he is able. Now, he is trying to teach me to totally and completely rely on him" (Dena Johnson Martin, *How Faith Leads to Trust*). The problem with this is we have to decide where to go from there.

Another problem is Christians can be just as bad as anyone when it comes to trustworthiness. It's sad, but it has certainly been attested to by some nauseatingly high statistics. Michael Slaughter says, "When we act out of conviction of heart, God combines our failures and victories together, and they become the will of God. You and I don't have to fear making mistakes. Integrity of heart is the first part of spiritual leadership."

Paul J. Meyer, in *Unlocking Your Legacy: 25 Keys for Success*, has a chapter entitled "Integrity—It's All You Are." He lists some of the traits that show just how real and measurable *integrity* is:

- Taking responsibility
- Keeping your word

- Being faithful in the little things
- Being honest
- Standing your ground for what is right
- Maintaining your honor and virtue
- Being morally upright
- Making right choices
- Never blaming others

Meyer goes on to say, "Integrity is also something you cannot pretend to have…If your foundation is integrity, your decisions will bear that out. If not, that too will become evident." Life challenges us with choices that confront us all the time. Without *integrity*, we probably have to spend an inordinate amount of time making a decision. That's not to suggest that every decision is an easy one; it means prayer is a part of each consideration. Some of them are easy to weigh on the scales of what is right.

Proverbs 20:21 (NIV) says, "An inheritance claimed too soon will not be blessed at the end." In other words, a fast buck may not be enough to last until the deal is done. I know a lot of situations, personal and otherwise, where negotiations fell apart because integrity was not a part of the transaction. There are also cases where deals are totally lost due to one of the parties being unwilling to *do the right thing*. Personally, life is too short to spend time trying to *get one over* on another person. I have turned down opportunities because the other party wasn't willing to act in good faith.

In the Introduction, I related a number of stories about my late wife and me. I didn't, however, share one that became very impactful in the middle of our lives together. I had noted that we were, in many ways, polar opposites. These differences weren't major, but they did provide a lot of heated conversation on occasion. Once, on the way to a meeting in Orlando with my wife driving, I asked if we could, once and for all, come up with a list of things we agreed on and those we didn't. The idea was to avoid confrontation over things that didn't matter and be able to spend the appropriate amount of time on the ones needing attention. You may be laughing at this point, but it was a serious endeavor. I made columns for what she liked on one side and for what I liked on the other. There was also a column in the middle for the ones we agreed on. This may be the point at which you fall out of your chair, picturing how this exercise went. I have a surprise for you if you are picturing her stopping the car and yelling at me straight on. In the end, the exercise concluded when we found that we had agreed on the importance of *integrity*. We knew there was no reason to go any further. The subject never came up again, but we did still have small disagreements every now and then.

David Steward, one of the founders of Worldwide Technologies and author of *Doing Business by the Good Book*, points out that a person's reputation is the most-valued asset he or she has. He writes that our example is what we pass on to future generations. My mother used to impress that on me at every turn. Does that sound familiar?

Integrity isn't something you are born with, and like trust, it can be lost and never regained. I believe integrity is at the foundation of any meaningful relationship. Going over the list above should provide insight into what it means to be trustworthy. This is not to say people of integrity don't slip occasionally. However, if there is a point at which you trip, a quick apology can go a long way at mending fences broken by the slip. People who have integrity are certainly to be considered trustworthy.

ADOPT A *WORLDVIEW* REFLECTING YOUR VALUES

In Chapter 2, we addressed the importance of *worldview*. While *worldview* transcends *community*, a true community will find it hard to function effectively unless the worldviews are essentially compatible. What we are basically looking for is a consistent set of values that reflects what we stand for. Competing worldviews will show the rest of the world who the adherents are and how they expect to reflect the essence of who they are.

Paradigms and worldviews have some common characteristics. Paradigms tend to box us in because they define the perimeters of our stated values. Worldview is much broader in that it provides the general scope of our belief system. When we consider the importance of integrity, we can then be able to firm up how we see the world.

In an article entitled "Worldview: Which Lens are You Looking Through?," Bob Burney, host of *Bob Burney Live*, WRFD Columbus, Ohio, points out that we all have a *worldview* whether we realize it or not. The *lens* through which we view the world is shaped by those things we have acquired by observation, learning, experience, etc. This is where worldview seems to look a lot like a *paradigm*. Whether it does or not, the point is that we all have biases we use to filter our view of life (or the world). These may not be true, but for the person who has a particular view, these filters determine how we act in certain circumstances.

Burney wrote, "When looking through the lens of a secular worldview, 'social justice' becomes the end-all answer to all of man's ills. Political activity and government programs take the place of spiritual transformation. After all, the only thing people need is a little bit of encouragement and a hand out to fan that 'spark of divinity' into a flame." Whether it is a political party or some organization with a cause, the members find the tenets of their position to be *trustworthy*.

If your values square with the Bible, you should consider how you want to formulate your worldview to reflect it. For us all, however, we need to be aware of the *creeping effect* of the secular worldview. G. K. Chesterton is famous for saying Christianity is not rejected because it lacks credibility. It has been hard to live by; so many just don't try. They would rather avoid the matter altogether. Living your life without giving thought to the important things is not a profitable endeavor.

You can find more in my first book, *The Dignity of Profit: Creating Community through Entrepreneurship*.

HAVE THE COURAGE TO SPEAK THE TRUTH

As pointed out in Chapter 1, truth may have different meanings to different people. Some people just expect others to lie and hope they can still benefit from the transaction. Others may want to try to structure a deal so tightly that their position is secure. Actually, neither of these is completely satisfying. There is another option, and it is the one that I usually end up taking. It is expecting the best from the person you are dealing with. Not that I recommend it, you understand. You have probably seen through the course of this book that it can end up bringing you a lot of heartburn.

If we are to be trustworthy, we must live in the realm of truth. Many are the folks who bought some line of something that doesn't even pass the *straight-face test*. We tend to put up with political advertising, and we expect sales and advertising people to "stretch the truth" somewhat. However, when it comes right down to it, nobody likes to be fooled. I know I hate it when someone calls on the phone and wants me to agree to something. If they are taping the conversation, it is for their benefit.

The conversation will probably not live until the call is over if you don't agree with them.

I'd be less than honest if I didn't share the fact that I have become unwelcome in settings where I speak up about an issue. Committees are the worst. They just want their members to go along with whatever they have already decided in many cases. You don't have to be disagreeable when you don't agree. If you are sincere about what you believe, you can hopefully win over right-minded folks. People who don't agree will probably not change their minds anyway. Your trustworthiness will come through when the outcome is clear. Don't look for praise, though. It's amazing how fast the folks who supported the other position can run away from any fallout.

Sometimes I'm not sure if it is courage driving me to speak up, but I think it is. My experiences in church meetings provide a long list of times when I chose to speak up on something that wasn't going in a good direction. In some cases, the pastor had a position he was holding on to, and I felt there were others in the group who really agreed with me. Amazingly, when I spoke out with a different approach to the matter, two very influential members spoke in favor of the recommendation I offered. At that point, the group joined in. It wasn't that I was just floating some notion I had just come up with. I had been in a similar situation at another church, and the direction I was supporting was very successful there. The dynamics were a bit different in this church, but the outcome was very much the same in the end. Of course, the pastor wasn't particularly pleased. I suppose we all tend to hold tight to our opinions when we feel we are right.

Edmund Burke wrote, "The only thing necessary for the triumph of evil is for good men to do nothing." There is a similar verse in the Bible, Proverbs 24:12. Now, I'm not suggesting you become contentious, but the truth is a powerful weapon to use against those who are not seeking to do what is not right. If we are to accept Jesus Christ as our standard, we only need to consider His statement in John 14:6 (NIV): "I AM the way, the *truth,* and the life; no one comes to the Father except through Me." His statements, in many cases, put Him in stark contrast with the powers of that day. Arguably, He was crucified because of His courageous attacks on the Pharisees and others. Stephen was stoned to death for his unwavering support of the truth (Acts 7:54–60).

You may be saying to yourself, *Do you expect me to subject myself to torture and/or death by speaking the truth?* That's certainly not my call. What I am saying is that the courage to speak up when appropriate comes from true faith in God and a sense of the timing you are facing.

When I was reading Michael Slaughter's book to get some input from it, I came across several notes my wife had written when she was reading it prior to going to a presentation. In a section entitled "Great Prayer," Slaughter had asked the question: "What if you knew that following Jesus Christ would cost you your life?" My wife reflected on the girl who was asked by one of the Columbine High School shooters about her faith. That girl was shot when she answered that she was a Christian. My wife's last note on this was, "Hope my life never becomes so important that I deny Christ."

I've never thought about it that way, and it was a window into her soul speaking to me from the *other side*. It's one thing to speak out, but it is another thing to give your life. It is recorded in Mark 8:35 that Jesus said, "For whoever would save his life will lose it, but whoever loses his life for My sake and the gospel's will save it." The interpretation of this is probably not as cut-and-dried as it might seem. Dr. John MacArthur, author of the study Bible I use, comments on this more as a choice to live your life focused on your own desires, etc., vs. a life lived for the sake of Christ and the Gospel. Perhaps your thought is *Oh, then I can do that*. Not so fast! You might want to consider what you would be willing to give up then. Think about my wife's comment.

I realize that this is tough talk. *Courage* is generally in short supply these days. It's hard to get anyone to stand up for something— even if it is something that they care about. A big part of what *The Dignity of Service* was about had to do with our own willingness to step out in faith. We all have a comfort zone, but it is not where we are called to live. I have written earlier in this book about *doing the right thing*. That's courage, and it doesn't always pay this side of heaven. A pastor friend of mine left his pulpit ministry because he needed to find out if he was in the right place. Shortly after that, his wife turned down a higher-paying job because of personal concerns. Today, he has gotten another job in a more suitable place, and his wife went into business for herself. Both of them are in a much better place now, but it took courage to take a hit financially. I'm also proud of her because I am a strong advocate of entrepreneurship where it is appropriate. The ethics are up to you then.

Rick Warren, in *The Purpose-Driven Life,* wrote, "God is not interested in your comfort; He is interested in your character." Part of our character is *trustworthiness*, and part of that is courage.

HAVE COMPASSION ON THOSE WHO ARE IN NEED

Compassion International says that "the meaning of compassion is to recognize the suffering of others and then to take action to help. Compassion embodies a tangible expression of love for those who are suffering." This might seem a bit far from the notion of *trustworthiness*, but it really isn't. Consider what Jeff Lyle wrote in *4 Steps for Helping Non-Believers Going Through Hard Times:* "All humans share one thing in common: we have all known pain and suffering on some level. Connect with them as a fellow human and offer them true compassion as you tell them how your own personal hope continues to rest in the Lord. You may simply be the gentle seed-planter during this season of struggle in the person's life. Be content with that. Planting and watering belong to us. Plant testimonial seeds of hope within them from your own life. God harvests those seeds later at the appropriate time."

The point is people trust those who have experienced the things they can relate to. I've seen it over and over again—illness, financial difficulties, marital struggles, or whatever—connecting with people who can authentically share their struggles makes all the difference in being able to relate to them.

I've been involved with the Walk to Emmaus movement for well over twenty years. This is an ecumenical organization similar to others, such as Cursio and Tres Dias. The focus is on helping Christians learn *progressive servanthood*. The power of these programs lies in the ability of the team members to connect with the pilgrims (those who are going through it for the first time). Another part of the Emmaus organization is called Kairos. This is for inmates in prisons. I fought going to be a part of it because I just didn't feel that it was my *thing*. I bet you have something in your background similar to it. Ultimately, I agreed to be a part of a team because the leader was someone I just couldn't turn down.

I know some people who work in prisons, specifically the one that I volunteered in. They were very critical of the program, saying the inmates just wanted to get out of their cells, or they liked the snacks they were given (who wouldn't?). My experience was that it didn't seem to be much of an issue. I got to know one of the inmates pretty well. We sat next to each other for the three days of the event. One day, when there was a particularly moving activity, he picked me up and gave me a bear hug. It was a little scary at first, but I quickly realized that he was genuinely expressing how the activity made him feel.

As I mentioned earlier, the key is having people as a part of the team who can relate to the inmates. Now, before you drive yourself nuts trying to figure out what I might have done, consider that some of us are *ringers*—basically faking it. OK, I wasn't really faking; I was basically there to show compassion. Most of these guys were *dead-enders*—they were not going home. I had a guy as a prayer partner who had killed someone. His wife gave birth after he was arrested, and then moved several states away. He had never seen his daughter because his wife wouldn't bring her to see him. I saw remorse first when he spoke of killing someone, and then I saw pain from not being able to connect to his daughter in any way. Those who had been in there for a long time seemed to have learned how to deal with their incarceration. Of course, these were in the group that came to the event. One of the folks I know who works there constantly speaks of how dangerous it is for the correctional officers. It is understandable that there has to be a different atmosphere with those who have to keep them in check. However, I would like to think there is some respect for people who volunteer to come and try to help them with their souls. It was the most amazing experience I have ever had.

I was asked to give a talk, and it was Christianity wrapped around a bit of my life story. I spoke of my mother, who died of Alzheimer's disease, but while I was in preparation for the event, my wife was diagnosed with a terminal Parkinson's-like condition. While some of them didn't have much for women, all of them had a mother. The lack of a relationship with their mother could have been the reason for them taking the wrong track in life. In any case, there was a connection with several of them.

MOST OF ALL, BE AN EFFECTIVE WITNESS TO YOUR FAITH

Do you think much about your *witness* as a Christian? If you happen to not be a Christian and you're wondering why you are still reading, perhaps you never had a thought about it. However, if you are a Christian, maybe you haven't thought about it either. For me, it never was a choice. Well, it always is, but my mother used to embarrass me into being good. Perhaps that's not exactly accurate, but she did hang a guilt trip on me when I was a teenager. It involved telling me that younger kids were watching me, and that I shouldn't lead them astray. Oh, how I hated that! I just wanted to be me. The other thing was her telling me, "Remember who you are." Of course, she meant that I shouldn't act like people who had no concern for their heritage. I mentioned earlier about how she harped on being a good example.

Our actions speak louder than our words, and we need to be very careful about how we conduct our lives.

I would love to tell you that she had such a profound effect on me that I never did anything that she wouldn't be proud of. This is a book about trust, and part of being trustworthy is telling the truth. It took me a long time to learn that being truthful is just part of being a trustworthy person. I mean, what's wrong with a *little white lie*? As mentioned earlier, John Wesley, the founder of what is now the United Methodist Church, said something to the effect that a lie is a lie regardless of the depth of it. My wife also helped me a lot with that. It just wouldn't be fair of me to not tell her the truth. She didn't always believe me, but that is another story.

Having waded through all we have about trust, there is a lot to try to get our minds around. I may have made it seem such an insurmountable challenge that you think no one can be that trustworthy. The fact is, we do fail many times every day. Thank God for His forgiveness, but we must go beyond that. It is incumbent on every Christian that they be as close to the ideal as we possibly can. Our model is the only perfect person who ever lived on this earth: Jesus Christ. We know that we can't be perfect, so what am I asking? Simply that you behave like a Christian should. If you do that, you will be an effective witness.

Michael Slaughter, in *Unlearning Church: Just When You Thought You Had Leadership All Figured Out,* wrote, "The world isn't interested in Christianity because we Christians aren't known as people who live what we say." Ouch! That really hurts. Do you agree? Don't you think that we Christians try to make our message fit what our audience wants to hear? It's not being true to our calling. Earlier I quoted G. K. Chesterton's famous statement about people not trying Christianity because it is hard. C. S. Lewis once said that we had inoculated Christians so that we can no longer catch anything. Pretty hard to be a witness when we don't feel like we need to be. All in all, our actions don't match our words, and that is *hypocrisy.*

Slaughter also wrote, "Pleasing God is the most important value I can model as a leader. When you live for the purpose of pleasing God, your life will honor God, bless and benefit others, and better than pleasure, bring you joy." In order to do that, we must understand how we *honor* God. I've thought for a long time that being untruthful to someone is like a slap in the face. It certainly doesn't honor God, and it doesn't attract others to be Christlike. "Your most important priority is to develop the spiritual person within you and then to allow your growth to influence others" (Slaughter).

In my book *The Dignity of Service: The Power of Social Entrepreneurship*, I wrote often of the need for Christians to be in service to others. This is how we show the love we have received from God and how we want to pass that on to others. David Steward points out that the primary role of a leader is to serve others. This means helping others succeed so they can grow to their full potential. The parable of the *Good Samaritan* (Luke 10:25–37) is an example of how we are to express and model God's love. This was such an outrageous notion for the Jews of that time, and yet, Jesus wanted to point out the importance of the act. We are *holy*, set apart for use by God. When we commit such audacious deeds, we have shown that being set apart should prompt us to act in a way that we demonstrate it. The notion of *community* seems to be under assault in today's culture. Expecting that we would behave as the Samaritan did seems foreign to us. Unfortunately, we live in times that cause us to be commuter workers, and that keeps us from interacting with others in a relaxed setting.

As we come to the end of this section, let me emphasize the uncommon manner in which we Christians are to behave. This is not to show off or in any way call attention to ourselves. We are to be the conduit through which God's love flows. In doing so, we will hopefully draw attention to the fact that we are followers of the Master. Giving glory to God is our primary focus, but we can be ready to respond to needs that God has made us aware of.

CHAPTER 11
Making the Connection to God

> Did I offer peace today? Did I bring a smile to someone's face?
> Did I say words of healing? Did I let go of my anger and resentment?
> Did I forgive? Did I love? These are the real questions. I must trust
> that the little bit of love that I sow now will bear many fruits, here in
> this world and the life to come.
>
> —Henri Nouwen,
> The Wounded Healer

What we do as believers when we seek to help others connect to God can be antithetical to how we evangelize people. As we will see in this chapter, we are not just to lead others to the church; we are to help them learn the importance of getting to know God. Our next step will then be to show them how serving others is the real way that we can help glorify God.

FROM TRUSTWORTHINESS TO DISCIPLESHIP

Trustworthiness is crucial to being a person of integrity. However, we haven't done our job as believers if we aren't focused on making disciples. Jesus didn't say in what is known as the *Great Commission* (Matt. 28:19–20) that we should "go therefore and *make church members*." Filling up the church rolls has a great appeal, but we can't stop at getting people to come to worship services once in a while. To me, a big part of trust is being able to share your story with others so that they will see what it is really like to be a Christian.

It took me a while to understand that showing up on Sundays periodically wasn't really our calling. In *The Dignity of Profit*, I spelled out the breadth of our *calling* as Christians. Every point is backed up with Scripture. No one gets off the hook. If we are to be sincere about being Christians, we must find how God wants to use us to help grow the Kingdom. Finding how you are wired up is a great place to start. This can easily be done by taking a Spiritual gifts assessment. Just knowing how you are gifted isn't enough, though. Putting your gift into action is how you can make a real impact.

So, what does it mean to be a disciple? At its most basic level, being a disciple means that you follow the opinions or teachings of another person. My thought is that it involves a much higher level of commitment. In a breakfast of eggs and bacon, the chicken is involved, but the pig is committed. A lot of us aren't in for that. We don't mind being involved, but that commitment thing is a bit over the line.

That's the problem with our culture, isn't it? We are so focused on ourselves that we just can't seem to give up much to anything that has a high level of commitment attached to it. Call it what you like, but Jesus asked us for that commitment. Buying a ticket so that you can get in to watch the show isn't the same as being a part of the event.

Several years ago, the idea of *entertainment evangelism* was making its way through the churches that were looking to infuse some excitement into their worship and programming. Many of us were skeptical, but we sort of put up with it for a while. Churches struggle today with how to get people interested in what they have to offer. Although it has been shown to be the wrong kind of measure, we still take attendance at worship services. Once, a beleaguered teacher told me that he was asked all sorts of questions in an attempt to find out how they were doing using some sort of measurement. The one question he said he wasn't asked was, "Are the students learning anything?"

Most of us like to be entertained or to at least have some excitement in what we are being subjected to. That's fine, of course, if you just need a break from the grind you have to endure. On the other hand, there's not much point in only moving from one presentation to the other. If you care about your job, your family, or your faith development, you are scratching your head over what tries to pass as a learning opportunity.

Michael Slaughter puts it this way: "We change the world by serving one person at a time, influencing one person at a time, and connecting one person at a time to God." Some of us want to have a big audience where many people take what we have to share with them and run with it. I suppose that happens, but relationships are made one at a time. Jesus seeks a personal relationship with us. It is our relationship, not someone else's. We each have a purpose, and we will know what that is if we seek to find how we are wired.

For many years, I have *mentored* people who needed direction in their lives. These weren't all situations that involved faith matters. However, if you really want to make a difference with people, you must lead them to the Word of God. Whether people want to acknowledge it or not, at the heart of every matter is how God wants us to react when we are confronted by it. Our purpose as Christians is to serve others to the glory of God. To me, that means serving by helping others find their direction in life. The specific way we are gifted gives us some guidance as to how we can best serve. I know of no better way to help make disciples than to introduce a person to how they are to live out their purpose.

> *The greatest persuasion point for the Unlearning leader is authentic life experience, not argumentative reasoning.*
> —Michael Slaughter

SEEKING COMMUNITY AS AN EFFECTIVE MEANS TO DRAW OTHERS CLOSER TO GOD

The subtitle of my first book is *Creating Community through Entrepreneurship*. My sources on how this works included Robert Lupton, author of *Toxic Charity: How Churches and Charities Hurt Those They Help (And How to Reverse It)*. His main point was that giving people something that they can and should be able to get for themselves creates a sense of dependency and takes away their dignity. In short, his program (and others that have chosen to use his methodology) is making a real difference in many areas. The key, as I see it, is that he is drawing the communities together rather than separating out the poor. The approach I am taking is to include as many members of the community as possible. Small businesses can be the backbone of a community, but everyone needs to be a participant in the process.

Another book that impacted my thinking dramatically was *Church on Sunday, Work on Monday: The Challenge of Fusing Christian Values with Business Life* by Laura Nash and Scotty McLennan. Their premise was there is a great need for business and professional people to be able to connect in a meaningful way with the church. I have read and written about this, and I believe they are correct. It is, in fact, the real impetus for my writing about this subject. Since 98 percent of the time for even regular churchgoers is spent outside of the church, how are we ever to make inroads into bridging the gap?

How in the world can we even dream of creating a sense of community if we can't get the various groups to try to tackle this problem? Rich and poor, lay and clergy, believer and nonbeliever, educated and uneducated, professional and blue-collar—these are the disparate groups that need to be a part of any community. Lupton is fairly successful in turning around communities that have been in decline for years. This hasn't been easy, and it sometimes is met with great resistance.

Christian Schwarz, creator of the Natural Church Development movement, uses carefully focused tests to help churches find their weak spots. The overall measure uses Eight Quality Characteristics to compare a specific church to the over eighty thousand churches they have worked with around the world. One of those characteristics is *Holistic Small Groups*. This is the one that relates to *community*. The test that is used to measure where the church or specific group lands on the scale is directed in such a manner as to help small groups ensure that the balance is in place that will allow the group to function effectively. In the larger context, this balance is critical. In a specifically targeted group, it is OK to lean toward the purpose of the group itself.

You can probably imagine how this can be used. While we want members of a group to be able to work together effectively, we don't want a bunch of zealots running around taking on all comers. If you have been in a church where people were at serious odds with each other, you know it's not a pretty sight. No organization can be operating at any level of efficiency if all the requisite parts are not seeking a common goal. Unfortunately, many of today's churches are just going through the motions. What happens in one committee is of no consequence to the others.

So, how do we draw people closer to God when we don't have any groups behaving in a harmonious manner? I'm not sure we are in many, many cases. It goes back to the problem of *self-centeredness*. If we are only out for ourselves, seeking only what is in our own benefit, how can we possibly expect to have anything that resembles community? There is no easy answer, but a solution is very necessary. My approach has been to try to put together groups that are totally focused on creating a true sense of community.

In a real sense, none of this stuff happens outside the ability of a group of people to have a passionate, intimate relationship with each other. God has some great things in store for those who are willing to take on the challenge. We grow when we find ourselves in the tough spots that make us rethink things. Our community must allow open discussion and honor the positions of its members. We are not all the same, and we do well to consider the power of working together for a common goal. The whole idea of community expressed means there can be a balance that enables us to be successful.

TRUSTING GOD TO HELP YOU LEAD OTHERS TO HIM

Christians should be able to understand that without God, we are nothing. Jesus was the greatest leader of all time, and He modified the skill of taking unprepared people and molding them into disciples. Michael Slaughter says that God's church "is most effective when leaders demonstrate Christ's light and life to each other." We can't just tell people what to do and expect the kind of response that is needed.

Our knowledge of God doesn't necessarily mean that we know Him. If we want to truly reach people, we need to make sure that the creation of a relationship comes from our own experience. Only a true relationship with Christ can be the foundation for a leader to develop other leaders. After all, there has to be a high level of trust developed between the leader and those he/she mentors. We can only teach what we know, but knowing God means a genuine experience in a relationship with Him.

In another sense, we can still have an issue with *worldview* when we seek to mentor others. We sometimes feel that we are all on the same page when we begin to talk about faith matters. As McLennan and Nash point out, there are worlds of difference between business/professional people and clergy when they begin to engage in discussing matters of faith. Besides the obvious *language* differences, the structures of the organizations have no commonality to the respective sides. It's hard to find the level of trust needed to engage in deep theological matters when you don't have the perspective of the other side. My experience has led me to believe it is much better to have dedicated laypeople who understand business to try to reach other businesspeople. Regi Campbell has written a book entitled *Mentor Like Jesus*.

This, as much as anything, chronicles his work mentoring "regular" business people in the format Jesus used to disciple His followers. He considers it as an extension of the movement Jesus started. Whatever it's called, it is a powerful way to pass on truth from one generation to another. A lot of this book has been about trying to find out how to avoid being led astray by deception. In 1 John 4:1–6, it exhorts believers to be very careful about false teachers and false prophets. Also, 2 Timothy 4:3–4 warns that *sound* teaching will give way to those who only will listen to what they want to hear. In a world where Facebook, Instagram, etc., are constantly being filled with people's opinions, many are succumbing to things that have very little to do with the truth.

Group discussions can be helpful to get conversations started, but it still requires a direct relationship in order to make a meaningful connection. As has been noted earlier, God is a god of relationships. It is what sets us apart from any other religious groups. Our experience has hopefully helped us to come to understand how God seeks that. When we are truthful with Him and open our hearts to Him, we can start building a relationship that works. The more we trust Him, the more He can trust us.

Regardless of how you recruit and train disciples, there has to be a follow-on where these people become leaders. This is so they can start the process anew. The mentoring Regi Campbell is doing is intended to have the disciples mentor others. This concept is most commonly known as *paying it forward*. This has actually been around for a long time. Basically, it is doing something for someone who is not expected to pay back the one who did something for him/her. Andrew Murray wrote that while many Christians do things out of gratitude, it's not what the giver intended. If someone did something for you and it wasn't paying you back, I would hope you felt that *paying it forward* would be a more appropriate thing to do. Murray went on to say that it isn't possible to pay someone back anyway. OK, maybe you could pay money back, but borrowing money creates an obligation to repay. There's nothing Christian about it, except you should repay debts. I've found that we are doing what God has called us to do when we offer unconditional love. Known as *agape* love, it follows the example of God offering love to humankind. Our purpose in life is to serve others to the glory of God. In that way, we do it out of love rather than obligation.

It is not in most of us to go out and try to seek out those who might be candidates for being led to God. It is also not appropriate in most cases. Evangelism is a spiritual gift, and we need to understand how that works. However, we can be part of the process by being sensitive to those who are exhibiting signs that they want to know more about our relationship with our Father God. We can be the one who plants the seed, or we can be the one who waters. We can also be the one who can see that someone else needs to be involved in reaching out to the seeker. However it works out, God will help you do your part, and He definitely wants you to step out in faith when you are called.

In order for us to be able to have a mentor-disciple relationship, we must be totally trustworthy. If we are doing this for some sort of self-aggrandizement, we have missed the point entirely. If we do not serve others to God's glory, it is self-serving and dishonors God. Maybe you need to refresh yourself on what it means to be a mentor if you aren't in it for the right reasons. Be sure to be prayerfully led to take on this important task before you step up and offer yourself.

TRUSTING THE SPIRIT TO PRODUCE THE FRUIT

I am the true vine, and my Father is the gardener. He cuts off every branch in me that bears no fruit, while every branch that does bear fruit he prunes so that it will be even more fruitful.

(John 15:1–2, NIV)

In *The Dignity of Profit*, I focused a lot on *outcomes*. Christians seem to have a problem with accountability because we are called to be faithful, not successful. If we are faithful, aren't we, in fact being successful in our part of the bargain? In the verses above, Jesus is telling his disciples that they are branches. Branches exist to provide the necessary nourishment for the fruit. If the branch is faithful, it will enable the fruit to be healthy and provide what it is intended to as well.

The title of this section speaks of *trusting the Spirit*. In Galatians 5:22–23, the *fruit of the Spirit* is said to include several things. As branches, we are to deliver the necessary ingredients to enable the Spirit to produce fruit. We can trust the fruit to be created if we do what we are called to do. If we receive and pass on what Jesus has given us, we will be faithful and enable the vine to produce the fruit it is supposed to. It is really the Spirit living in us that makes this possible because Jesus gave it to us.

Right before the fruit of the Spirit is addressed in Galatians 5, there is a list of those things that are *of the flesh*. These, of course, are not of the Spirit. We cannot be trustworthy if we do the fleshly things contrary to the Spirit. When we do, we have closed the Spirit off from the ability to produce the fruit it is to do.

So, the way that we can help the Spirit beyond our own situation is to show others the *fruit* that comes because of our faithfulness. If we are successful in doing so, we will be helping others to produce their own fruit. Whether this is in the setting of being a mentor or if it is just your being a witness by the way you live your life, your trustworthiness can be a major factor in helping others to see the *Way*.

As sort of a footnote in this discussion about connecting people to God, I would like to say a bit about the concept of *multiplication* as it relates to spreading the Kingdom of God. There have been several good books written by people who have been successful in bringing large numbers to Christ. Some of these are church planters, and that seems to make sense. Sometimes, it comes across as multilevel marketing—something like Amway, where you recruit others who, in turn, recruit others. The concept can be very powerful, but there are other ways to accomplish similar results.

Regi Campbell and Michael Slaughter have been quoted here, and they have success in more traditional ways. It's not that we don't want as many to come to Christ as possible; that was mentioned earlier. If people are coming because they have some kind of emotional attraction, it is often the case that they will drift away at some point. My experience has been that we should make ourselves available in the event we encounter others who are at that flash point in their faith journey. It's amazing what we can accomplish if we follow the challenge of 1 Peter 3:15 (NIV): "Always be prepared to give an answer to everyone who asks you to give the reason for the hope that you have. But do this with gentleness and respect." Oh, by the way, it is imperative that you are trustworthy in your approach to life. Nothing can be more devastating than to make a great connection with someone, and then find out you are a phony. In that case, you are in it for yourself, and it becomes apparent very quickly.

Keep your lives free from the love of money and be content with what you have, because God has said, "Never will I leave you; never will I forsake you." (Heb. 13:5, NIV)

CHAPTER 12
Getting Beyond Self

> *There is one thing that you can trust everybody to do, and that is to put his interest above yours.*
>
> —Milton Friedman,
> 1976 Nobel Memorial Prize in Economic Sciences

For me, I wanted to write this book for a couple of reasons. One, I was hoping to get some catharsis to soothe my wounds from my business career. In that respect, that reason was fulfilled. The other one was that I wanted to help others find a way to deal with (or live with) the jungle of nefarious characters that seem to be flooding the world of business. When I call these *business* matters, I am referring to both personal and career situations. My readership will determine whether I have been successful in the second reason.

There is actually another thing that I wanted to accomplish. I really wanted to see if there was such a thing as a book about trust that didn't have God as the only real answer. I was not successful at that, and I am very pleased it turned out that way. I knew in my heart it would be that way, and perhaps it influenced my research. On the other hand, I have a great deal of experience to back up my beliefs. As I wrote earlier, there is no way that it can be proven either way, but experience convinced me that God does work in our lives (see Romans 8:28).

Our challenge is this: we have to work with people, and there has to be some level of trust. Nothing upsets me more than to have people promise to do something and not do it. There are, of course, instances where circumstances get in the way. This bothers me so much that I just hate to have to tell someone that I didn't get something done that I said I would.

In a real sense, the actual problem may be a *leadership failure* when it gets past the individual level. The project I mentioned earlier that shut down is a victim of unfulfilled promises. The ministerial alliance agreed to support it, or I wouldn't have even dreamed of taking it on. In fact, they were the lynchpin that made it happen. Once we embarked on it, I was asked what I needed from them. My answer was volunteers to work the café, and young people to be trained by the volunteers. We got very few of each. Sadly, we were able to make the required number of trainees, but the lack of volunteers caused a lack of support from the community at large. When I discussed it with a board member who was also a part of the alliance, he said that the pastors couldn't get their congregations to participate. I'm too embarrassed to share the actual response that one of the pastors got. It's pretty clear to me that God is in the writing of the book.

I actually started on another book several years ago, but it seems to have gotten lost. Anyway, I got on the path of *dignity* on my first book and used it again on the second one. Stratton Press actually approached me about a rewrite of *Profit*, but I really didn't want to do it. I hope you will read it, but I recommend that you read *Service* first. It is more focused and will give some direction about *Profit* that will make it clearer to you.

The real irony in *Trust* is that it has come at the time of the project I just shared. Hopes were high when *Profit* was written, and I hoped that *Service* would appeal to a wider audience.

The *elephant in the room* turned out to be *apathy*. Many people applauded the vision that went into the project, but in the end, the support just wasn't there. Maybe I was expecting too much, but it seems pretty apparent that most people just don't want to be followers. In this case, it may be that they don't want to be leaders either. In a documentary I watched about the Kennedys, the comment was made that Ted didn't want to be president, but he didn't want anyone else to be either. That makes me feel a little better because it would mean that it wasn't about me.

It would be rare to find an extremely large group of folks out there that have not had a broken trust that they have had to deal with. Let me know if you are one or know someone who is. The most vulnerable categories seem to be young, inexperienced folks, widows or widowers who are left with tasks they hadn't had to deal with, and the elderly who are finding themselves in tight financial spots or are unable to make good decisions at this point in their lives. I haven't addressed the notion of punishment for the perpetrators of the deceptions that have been done to their victims. There has been too much of my Christian faith displayed for me to launch into something in the way of retribution for them. After all, we are called to forgive, aren't we? (Matt. 6: 14–15).

It seems the nature of these offenses runs the gamut of organizations or individuals. There have been some large companies shut down on account of their crimes and deception. On the other hand, there have been folks operating out of their basements or wherever as well. Many of these deceptions aren't attractive enough for lawyers or government agencies to go after. I happen to be one of those people who feel it is my calling to take on anything affecting people who are helpless and can't do anything about what has happened to them.

I once decided to change my cell phone carrier at the end of December. It's a crazy time, I know, but the contract was about to be up on one that I had purchased on a special deal. Since I was to be traveling during the time the previous contract was ending, I wanted to get ahead of the game by setting everything up ahead of time. All seemed to go well until I got to the point of agreeing for the new carrier to take over my phone number. I didn't even realize what had happened until I tried to let my previous carrier know to make the switch. My online access was shut down, but I didn't realize that it meant that the contract had been terminated early.

I got a bill from the previous carrier for an early termination fee of $120. Mind you, this was six days early. It's a long story, but I was not going to pay that fee. I got a person in the legal department who could only repeat that they had the right to charge the fee. I ended up with a vice president of marketing (at least that's what I believe happened). He wasn't very helpful, but I finally told him that I had been in sales for most of my working life. I said that I would never do that to a customer of mine. There was a pause, and he said he would get back to me. Finally, they agreed to charge me for the six days and waive the fee. That's all I wanted in the first place.

I suppose this falls under the category of *poor direction*, but it would have been costly if I had to pay the fee. On the other hand, I look at this as not caring enough to do the right thing. There have been many of these instances for me, and I would expect that there are for others. I realize that I can be a bit fractious at times, but a lot of my experience has been with customer service. Almost every day, I find some ridiculous example of a representative just not caring about the customer. I had grown accustomed to bureaucratic organizations making rules designed to benefit them. Many larger organizations now seem to do the same thing. Very small, mom-and-pop businesses are sometimes worse.

So, I guess where I want to go with this is to explore the notion that there can be something deeper here. Is it possible to be outstanding at serving others to the point that you can make your business or organization an example of how it should be done? If so, is it what you want to do, or is it just not worth the trouble? When I used to do promotional retail sales, I just couldn't abide by the lack of concern for the customer. OK, many of the sales were store closings, and everyone gets a bit contentious in those settings. Part of my job was to enable the store owner to keep the necessary number of employees to be able to finish the sale without wearing them down. From my standpoint, owners would want to cancel our sale early if we did too good of a job, or it was costing them too much to keep going.

Part of my problem might just be that I focus too much on the customer. I've done my share of killing a sale because I just didn't see that it was what the customer needed. On the other hand, I always felt that I had a responsibility to customer and retailer. The customer should be treated with respect since they are spending money in the store. The retailer is always walking a tightrope when it comes to being able to do business the right way versus going broke. I have to admit that I have been in stores where everything defied logic. In several cases, the store would be dirty, the employees were surly, and the inventory wasn't that appealing. However, the business did a lot of business because they knew how to keep the customer satisfied. It created a level of trust that was very satisfactory to customers.

Michael Slaughter says that God has woven into us the desire for significance. If that is true (and I believe it is), we should want to do a good job to be a trustworthy person. I've heard it said that even at five years old, we are aware that we want to make a difference. Being trustworthy certainly fits that bill. When you look at the progression that I put forth in part II about *obstacles*, there are a lot of folks who aren't doing much to make a positive difference.

Have you ever been watching a true crime show on TV and wondered why in the heck some people spend so much time doing wrong? They must either have no conscience, or they live on antacid. I was watching one recently where a man went out to collect a debt and was killed, cut into pieces, and dumped in the river in garbage bags. I don't know how much the debt was, but the man ended up spending thirty-five years in prison. I just don't see the balance of value versus cost. On the other hand, the killer gets to be taken care of by the state.

WHERE IS COMMUNITY IN ALL THIS?

Just about all of what I have put forth had to do with people who did something wrong. I did mention in the beginning about people just being lazy or not caring. The churches I know of are full of members who just don't do very much. It's not that they are bad people, per se; somehow, they just don't see service as important. On several occasions in the book, I have pointed out that our purpose is to serve others to the glory of God. Never let it be said that I don't speak openly about my opinions, but what passes for concern is pretty lame in many cases.

In *The Dignity of Profit*, I spent a lot of time pointing out that we do *good* things for people without considering how that affects them. We think that giving a needy person something is going to make them grateful. It probably should, but taking away their dignity pours cold water on the matter. In *The Dignity of Service*, Jeff Baker and I sought to make a big point about how to figure out what service each person should undertake. In the end, all three of these books have been aimed at building a sense of community. We're in this together, folks. By supporting one another and being trustworthy, people can be major factors in strengthening your community.

I just came off a project that was designed to help get Christians in this particular area interested in helping their communities avoid drying up and blowing away. There was a lot of potential, but the folks just didn't express much interest in turning things around. Now, an out-of-town group has gotten the main city to put out a lot of money to get this outdoor group to come in. This has the potential to provide a big boost to the tourist trade. At this point, it seems like people are doing all sorts of things that are very self-serving. It will be interesting to see how this unfolds. If they can get businesses from outside of the area to come in and set up shop, it may be the boost that it is purported to be. Meanwhile, the notion of knitting together a community out of this doesn't offer much promise.

At this point, we are coming off a very contentious election season. It is probably pretty well settled, but there is still a lot of wrangling over voting irregularities. All the while, the polarization of the country keeps getting worse. Trustworthiness seems a faraway concept since the divided camps of the two major political parties are very focused on their own agendas. Even simple matters seem to become *bones of contention*. The pendulum swings farther to the extremities each time these elections are held. The *middle* is not necessarily a great place to be, but some common ground would be welcome. Rather than making progress, we just seem to have more and more exhumations of past positions.

A lot of this is the result of the outflow of young people from rural areas. Most areas find themselves losing them to college first and then taking jobs elsewhere, or they simply hang around and mostly don't amount to much. There are certainly jobs that can be comfortably filled by the locals, but it seems that the middle class in rural areas may be fading away. The people who move in from other areas seem to locate in areas where they can escape urban sprawl or just want to buy some property to retire on. Property values don't increase because the houses are very well taken care of. Factories aren't moving to these areas much because the level of trained workers doesn't meet their needs.

The point about trust here has to do with the lack of concern about the rest of the community. The ministerial alliance is not very active in most areas, and they can't seem to understand that they should be a leading factor in strengthening the local area. They wouldn't dare get involved in the economy, and they just seem to become more and more inbred. Trying to get young people into the churches is not a productive activity. More and more rural areas are seeing retail businesses go to larger areas nearby or to online retailing. It is a vicious cycle. The lack of involvement of governmental officials doing anything to change things doesn't make a pretty picture.

SO WHAT IS THE CHALLENGE?

Specifically, the need is to get people involved. The lack of interest in many communities is palpable. There are some beautiful areas in rural countryside, but getting people to move to them is less of a challenge than getting them to move where a community can develop. Organizations that should be charged with community development are just not very active due to a lack of interest. As more and more of the people who once ran these cities and towns die or move away, hanging on is becoming even more of a challenge.

I've studied some of the *multiplication* materials that suggest (and have been proven in some cases) that Jesus's design of *making disciples* was the original plan. It's hard to argue with that, but why isn't it working in a big way? As I finish the third of my books about *community*, I have to go back to the notion that relationships can develop when people get together as a community. There has to be trust (see Chapter 2), or there aren't relationships. This has been mentioned in several different ways throughout the book, and that is by design. The relationship that God calls us to is quite different from any other religion.

So this can turn into multiplication, but it still needs the one-on-one approach to happen. If one connects with one, the second one can do the same. If the first one does it again, there is certainly multiplication going on. However, this is not Amway or whoever. It shouldn't flow to the top—at least to a specific person other than Christ. Most of this has been about church planting, and it starts to take on the flavor of bureaucracy. I'm all for connectionalism— churches drawn together by similarity of style of worship, doctrine, etc.—because it helps us clarify who we are. However, as I have experienced with the twenty-seven churches that are members of the ministerial alliance I worked with, they just don't care to work with the others. I don't think this is that rare.

At the risk of suggesting we *reinvent the wheel*, my sense is that this has to be reduced to the community level. It almost has to be in an area large enough to have some homogeneity in neighborhoods. Even then, our mobile society militates against being able to make this work for the long run. So what am I saying? Well, I took my cue from some of those who took it on as a local church. Some very creative situations have worked well. Here are some of them:

- A church in Dallas turned some vacant space into a place for those who needed an area to do computer work. It is no charge, and they expect that the people who come there are those who would ever think about coming to church.
- A group managed to get some land donated to build a strip shopping center. The anchor was a café with clearly the mission of providing a place for faith development to happen in the real world. It has since expanded to other businesses that are faith-based.
- A drive-through building with a small outdoor seating area sells coffee, baked goods, etc., and gives a *blessing* to patrons as they pass through. Most of the workers are physically or mentally impaired. Proceeds go to help those who are impacted by a home fire, flood, or other disaster.
- Some girls in a church group created a company that made jewelry, which they sold at a mall in a kiosk. Their proceeds went to help the homeless in the area. The concept was shown at a regional conference and replicated in another city.

- Luke 16 Corp (the nonprofit that I founded) is undertaking a new project designed to foster *social entrepreneurship* projects in predominantly rural towns where the need is great. These projects are planned for local support so that entrepreneurial ventures will have a better chance of succeeding. You can reach us via email at luke16corp@outlook.com.

The common denominator in all these is that they were a group formed for the specific purpose of using locals to put together a means of reaching out to the community. Some are nonprofit, and some are for-profit. Some use volunteers, and some have a mix of both. They do provide a venue for sharing their faith stories. This is life at its most meaningful state. You can't script them for the most part. They happen because it is the convergence of faith and human need. It is the need to do something significant.

My nature is to be an explorer. I used to love it as a lad of ten or eleven. Much of what my friends and I discovered wasn't new, but surely there were times when we happened on something *different*. I now have property on almost twenty-three acres in the Ozarks. I have walked it a few times, mostly over the same paths. If there is foliage that has grown since my last visit, I marvel that it has probably not been seen by another human. It's not remarkable, but it is amazing in many ways. What makes it so is that God created that plant, but it may not seem to have a purpose. In all likelihood, it will at least be able to reproduce itself somehow. If it does, it may serve to feed a deer or some other animal that wanders by. Surely, God planned that, just as surely as He provides for us. His providence is one of His most trustworthy purposes, I would think.

> *Because of the LORD's great love we are not consumed, for his compassions never fail. They are new every morning; great is your faithfulness.*
> (Lam. 3:22–23, NIV)

I began this book writing about the things that we need to be able to trust. I then waded through the myriad of possible pitfalls we face. Learning how to deal with the obstacles was next. What followed was my way of conveying the need to understand just how important it is to trust God. My way of achieving that has probably been a little clunky.

It's not easy to explain things that are, in some ways, unexplainable. This effort is my way of helping make the transition from thinking about trusting to actually being able to do it.

In a real sense, life would be a bit nutty if we spent an inordinate amount of time trying to evaluate each situation to determine if we can really trust our assessment of it. On the other hand, wandering around willy-nilly doesn't make any sense either. So here's my way of dealing with the quandary we are in: prepare yourself for each new opportunity by learning to trust God.

Dr. John MacArthur is a clergyman, an author, a radio and TV personality, and president of Grace Theological Seminary. He was once asked if he ever veered off the path of the *straight and narrow.* His answer was no, and he went on to say that because he is walking with God, the Spirit wouldn't let it happen. Realizing that he is a Calvinist, you might immediately conclude that it is his belief in *predestination* that caused him to feel that way. That's not the way I see it. Again, Romans 8:28 gives us great comfort when we are in the arms of Christ.

This is not to say that we are merely marching along like robots. I truly believe that we have free will. However, staying connected to God opens the door for the Spirit to help us stay focused. It may not even come up on our radar screen, but we are being guided nonetheless. For a long time, I fought against the notion that someone else had that much control over me. It still comes up at times, but God's grace also reaches in to *keep me busy* until I pick up the path again. It used to frustrate me mightily, but I am being reinforced daily so that I become aware of what is happening.

It is my sincere hope that you have been blessed in some way by all this. It has been one of the most enlightening things I have ever done. Research has always been my main way of exploring, and the results have opened new doors for me. This is probably the last in the *Dignity* series, but then again, I thought I was through after *Profit*.

Please share any stories that you want. I'll be writing a periodic newsletter to be able to offer fresh stories and thoughts. Take advantage of it.

Also, I have cited many references, and these are listed at the end. They can all be found on the Internet, and I hope you will check some of them out. There are some particularly interesting stories that may be something you can be encouraged by. Speaking of encouragement, one of my very favorite passages in the New Testament is *1 Thessalonians 5:11a (NIV)*: "Therefore encourage one another and build each other up." It has been my experience that we Christians have a responsibility to be encouraging, for our life struggle is arduous in many ways. Knowing that we can relate to one another and work together to make it through these struggles can lighten our load and keep us focused on our purpose.

> *And we know that in all things God works for the good of those who love Him, who have been called according to His purpose.*
> *(Rom. 8:28)*

APPENDIX A
Jobs Where Trust Was Broken

From a business standpoint, the incidents were seemingly boundless. Here are the most noteworthy ones:

1. My first partner in business turned out to be in deep debt with the bank that we chose to work with. Because of his inability to provide his portion of the initial funds, we got into pretty serious trouble early in our operation. The other scam was the bank who was trying to make their customer (my partner) whole by using me. They went so far as to make a false report to the credit bureau in order to have other unsuspecting potential investors/creditors thinking that he was OK.
2. My next *mishap* was with the employer I worked for after the business in item 1. I was promised a department head position, but it took so long that I never really got underway in the job. Fortunately, a new opportunity came along that gave me the ability to move on.
3. My next job after that was one that I really enjoyed. It involved every aspect of the products and services I was responsible for. After a couple of years, my pay structure was changed so that I was making about half as much, and I moved on again. This was after I had doubled the department's sales in eighteen months.
4. I never really got going at the next job. I was promised the territory that would include my current home. Instead, I spent four days a week or more in another state, and I never made any money. A job that I had wanted for a while became available. That company went under a couple of years later.

5. Two weeks into the new job, the company I went to work for merged with another company. On its face, it seemed to be a much better opportunity. However, the merger didn't last, and I was back with the original company. That would have been OK, except they began to reduce the sales force. Due to my tenure with the original company, I was offered an independent contractor arrangement. It worked pretty well, and I was enjoying newfound freedom to work where I felt I could be most effective. The company couldn't stand my success and tried to cut me out of a major sale. I threatened to sue, and a settlement was arranged. I had to leave.

6. During the time that I was an employee with the company noted in item 5, I purchased a Mail Boxes, Etc. (MBE) franchise to be a supplement to my income. I had a manager running it, which would have worked OK if I had made any money after I left that company. I tried a couple of things that individually didn't work out, but both led to better things. One of them was the job I took, which is cited in item 7.

7. Next, I took a job that meant a move to St. Louis. It also meant that I had to sell the MBE store. The original plan was to be in Alabama, and my wife never forgave me for that. It wasn't my fault, and the ultimate outcome was very good for us—for a time. That company ended up in bankruptcy and sold out to a competitor. I could have stayed, but I didn't trust the new owners.

8. One of the main reasons for the bankruptcy was the infighting between family members. There were also many product liability lawsuits that caused a major hit in the cash flow. I had started a side business during the bankruptcy time and went on to do that full-time when the bankruptcy was final. I lost about $10,000 from the bankruptcy, which was for travel expenses that I had paid.

9. My new business was my own manufacturing operation, and it went well for several years. Unfortunately, suppliers and contract businesses were trying to suck the life out of my business, and I had to sell out to the one most favorable to me. The owner of that company died, and the business was sold to a very unscrupulous person. He lied to me about several things that started the beginning of the end of our relationship. I moved most of the business I could to another principal. That,

too, came to the same kind of end after a few years. I decided to give it up at that point.

10. During this time, I had begun teaching at the college level. One of the textbooks was describing how business brokers worked. I mentioned it to my wife, and she said that it was a perfect fit for me. The organization I ended up with made us become members of a network for brokers. My wife and I went together to the initial presentation, and she was taken in by the sales pitch that the owner made. I was doubtful as well, but I felt that even a much smaller amount of expected revenue would be good. It didn't work out, but I was able to purchase a business from another member. I still have that business eighteen years later.

11. My son-in-law and a business broker, with whom I had worked, bought a business together. We had a purchase-money mortgage on the sale. The sellers pulled a fast one on us by having a brother stay with the business and sabotaging the sale. We ended up shutting down the business in less than eleven months. The brother started his own business and took all our customers. We were left in deep debt.

12. One day, when I was looking for something in my filing cabinet, I came across a solicitation that I had received from a company that did promotional sales for retail businesses. The company was looking for former business owners who wanted to join them as consultants. The file included mailings I had started getting when I had my own retail business over twenty years earlier. It was perfect timing. I hadn't had the ability to take off and travel like the job involved until that day. I jumped at it and worked for the company for almost six years. I did reasonably well, but the owner didn't see it that way. He didn't have much choice but to hire me when I joined his organization because no one else that applied wanted to relocate. Once he found someone to replace me, he found it very easy to renege on what we had agreed to. I did make a lot of money when I had that job, and I picked up a couple of sales on my own later.

Now, I wouldn't want to leave you with the notion that all these instances were negative experiences. Far from it. It is my belief that God has been in all of them, and I came out better with every circumstance. I didn't always feel that it was the case, but we can only understand life by looking back on it. I wish that for all of you if you will only surrender to His plan for your life.

APPENDIX B
Two Real Stories about Trusting

Both the stories described below actually happened in a medium-sized city in the heart of the Mississippi Delta. It is, in fact, where two of my children were born and where I started my first *real* entrepreneurial company.

The first story is about a long-established manufacturing company that sold their products nationally in the hardware industry. It was one of those very stable businesses that hired a lot of local people and paid them well. Not everyone wants to work in a factory, so it wasn't like people were standing in line to go to work there. However, the fact that the company was so well known made it attractive to those who saw it as a long-term situation.

One day, along came a group from New York State that expressed some interest in purchasing the company. I don't recall all the details, but the deal went through. In the end, however, the new owners cleaned out the company and left town. The company never recovered from that scam.

The other story was one that I knew pretty well. This, too, was a well-established business, but it catered to more local customers. It was not an upscale sort of business; their skills were more in the way of welding. One family had owned it forever, it seemed, and the business still carried the name. A somewhat flamboyant couple decided to purchase the company, and they began to make lots of changes. Oh, these weren't changes to manufacturing; they made cosmetic changes and changes to the employee benefits—physical ones, that is.

When I opened my store, I decided to create the true atmosphere of a home-building business. Among other things, I built what I referred to as a *corral*. The purpose of this was to have a place for customers to come up with their ideas, and we would help flesh them out. We used faux building items to simulate a house (of sorts). I admit that I was rather proud of it. So when the new owners of the manufacturing business came in and admired it, my pride led to selling them the entire structure.

A few days later, some of the factory workers came and took away my creation. They also purchased a lot of other items for their build-out as well. By the way, I did get paid for it. After perhaps a couple of months, my wife and I got an invitation to see the reveal of their new facilities. I was shocked! It was hard to believe what they had done to the place. However, it was even harder to imagine what they had spent on such an extravagance. Now, you may be ahead of me, but the business closed due to them running out of money with which to operate the factory.

So here's my question. Do you agree that both of the stories had to do with trusting? Personally, I do, since there was unwarranted trust placed on both of the new owners. I don't know if other people got paid as I did from the second company. Nonetheless, the employees and vendors got hurt because their livelihoods were adversely affected. I recently visited that city for the first time in many years. I didn't notice any of the factories that were there when I was. I'm not suggesting that the two stories were the cause, but people get dispirited when they see the fabric of their communities ripped apart by untrustworthy people. Of course, they bear a lot of the blame themselves.

REFERENCES

Adler, Mortimer. American philosopher, educator, and popular author.

Austin, Lynn. American author of many Christian fiction novels and holds the record for most Christy Awards won: eight.

Begg, Alistair. American pastor. Truth for Life Ministries (truthforlife.org).

Berra, Yogi. American professional baseball catcher, who later took on the roles of manager and coach.

Bloom, Linda, and Charlie. Trained as psychotherapists and relationship counselors, they have worked with individuals, couples, groups, and organizations since 1975.

Burke, Edmund. Irish statesman, economist, and philosopher. Burney, Bob. Founded and pastored Calvary Baptist church in

Westerville, Ohio, until 2000, when he was called to host Bob Burney Live on the Word radio in Columbus, Ohio.

Campbell, Regi. Entrepreneur, writer, and mentor. He was involved in the founding of fifteen companies, serving as CEO four times.

Chesterton, G. K. English writer, philosopher, lay theologian, and literary and art critic. He has been referred to as the prince of paradox.

Chua, Amy, and Jed Rubenfeld. October 2018. "The Threat of Tribalism," *The Atlantic*. TheAtlantic.com.

Compassion International. American child sponsorship and Christian humanitarian aid organization headquartered in Colorado Springs, Colorado, that aims to positively impact long-term development of children living in poverty globally.

Covey, Stephen. American educator, author, businessman, and keynote speaker. His most popular book is *The 7 Habits of Highly Effective People*.

Disney, Walt. American entrepreneur, animator, writer, voice actor, and film producer.

Eberstadt, Nicholas. 2006. *Men Without Work: America's Invisible Crisis*. West Conshohocken, Pennsylvania: Templeton Press.

Evans, Tony. American Christian pastor, speaker, author, and widely syndicated radio and television broadcaster in the United States.

Freud, Sigmund. Austrian neurologist and the founder of psychoanalysis.

Friedman, Milton. American economist and statistician who received the 1976 Nobel Memorial Prize in Economic Sciences for his research on consumption analysis, monetary history, and theory, and the complexity of stabilization policy.

Goethe, Johann W. von. German poet, playwright, novelist, scientist, statesman, theatre director, critic, and amateur artist.

Herbert, Frank. American science-fiction author best known for the 1965 novel *Dune* and its five sequels.

Ingram, Chip. Christian pastor, author, teacher, founder, teaching pastor, and CEO of Living on the Edge Ministries.

Irving, John. American-Canadian novelist and screenwriter.

Johnson, Samuel. English writer who made lasting contributions to English literature as a poet, playwright, essayist, moralist, literary critic, biographer, editor, and lexicographer.

Keller, Timothy. American pastor, theologian, and Christian apologist. He is the chairman and co-founder of Redeemer City to City, which trains pastors for ministry in global cities.

Lee, Robert E., American Confederate general best known as a commander of the Confederate States Army during the American Civil War.

Lewis, C. S. British writer and lay theologian. Referred to as was one of the intellectual giants of the twentieth century and arguably one of the most influential writers of his day.

Lupton, Robert. Founder, Focused Communities Strategies (fcsministries.org).

Lyle, Jeff. Creator of Transforming Truth Ministry (transformingtruth.org).

MacArthur, Dr. John. American pastor and author known for his internationally syndicated Christian teaching radio and television program *Grace to You*.

Manning, Brennan. 2005. *The Ragamuffin Gospel: Good News for the Bedraggled, Beat-Up, and Burnt Out*. Multnomah: Crown Publishing Group.

Martin, Dena Johnson. Founder of Dena Johnson Ministries, a nonprofit corporation aimed at helping others find beauty through a broken life.

Merton, Thomas. American Trappist monk, writer, theologian, mystic, poet, social activist, and scholar of comparative religion.

Meyer, Paul. 2003. *Unlocking Your Legacy: 25 Keys for Success*. Chicago, Illinois: Moody.

Murray, Andrew. South African writer, teacher, and Christian pastor. Considered missions to be the chief end of the church.

Nash, Laura and Scotty McLennan. 2001. *Church on Sunday, Work on Monday, The Challenge of Fusing Christian Values with Business Life*. Hoboken, New Jersey: Jossey-Bass.

Nouwen, Henri. Dutch Catholic priest, professor, writer, and theologian. His interests were rooted primarily in psychology, pastoral ministry, spirituality, social justice, and community.

Paiget, Jean. Swiss psychologist best known for his work on child development and education.

Pascal, Blaise. French mathematician, physicist, inventor, philosopher, writer, and Catholic theologian.

Penney, James Cash. Founder, JCPenney retail chain.

Pritchard, Ray. President of Keep Believing Ministries, that includes a national preaching ministry, outreach to China, and other goodwill efforts.

Rackham, Neil. 1988. *SPIN Selling*. New York City: McGraw-Hill Education.

Reagan, Ronald. Fortieth US president.

Robinson, Kara Mayer. Host, moderator, celebrity interviewer, established journalist, and Columbia University–trained psychotherapist.

Schlessinger, Dr. Laura. American talk radio host and author. *The Dr. Laura Program* is heard weekdays for three hours on Sirius XM Radio.

Schwarz, Christian. German author, lecturer, and researcher. He is the founder and president of Natural Church Development (NCD International).

Shakespeare, William. English playwright, poet, and actor, widely regarded as the greatest writer in the English language and the world's greatest dramatist.

Slaughter, Michael. Served for nearly four decades as the lead pastor and chief dreamer of Ginghamsburg and the spiritual entrepreneur of ministry marketplace innovations. Creator of Passionate Churches, LLC.

St. Augustine of Hippo. Bishop of Hippo from 396 to 430, one of the Latin Fathers of the Church, and perhaps the most significant Christian thinker after St. Paul.

Stanley, Charles. *Walking in the Favor of God*. American pastor. In Touch Ministries, Sermon notes (intouch.org).

Steward, David. American businessman, chairman, and founder of World Wide Technology, one of the largest African-American– owned businesses in America. Author of *Doing Business by the Good Book*.

Swindoll, Charles "Chuck." Pastor and author. Insight for Living Ministries (insight.org).

Thomas, Clarence. Associate Justice of the Supreme Court of the United States.

Tozer, A. W. American Christian pastor, author, magazine editor, and spiritual mentor.

Trump, Donald. Forty-fifth US president.

Warren, Rick. American Baptist evangelical Christian pastor and author. He is the founder and senior pastor of Saddleback Church, which is one the largest megachurches in the United States.

Washington, Booker T. American educator, author, orator, and adviser to several presidents of the United States.

Watson, Thomas J. IBM CEO who guided the company to great success.vv

Wesley, John. English cleric, theologian, and evangelist, who was a leader of a revival movement within the Church of England known as Methodism.

Zacharias, Ravi. Ravi Zacharias International Ministries (Rzim.org).

Zimbardo, Philip. 2007. *Lucifer Effect: Understanding How Good People Turn Evil*. New York City: Penguin Random House LLC., Rider.

www.ingramcontent.com/pod-product-compliance
Lightning Source LLC
Chambersburg PA
CBHW052032030426
42337CB00027B/4966